# Physical Characteristics of the Parson Russell Terrier

(from The Kennel Club breed standard)

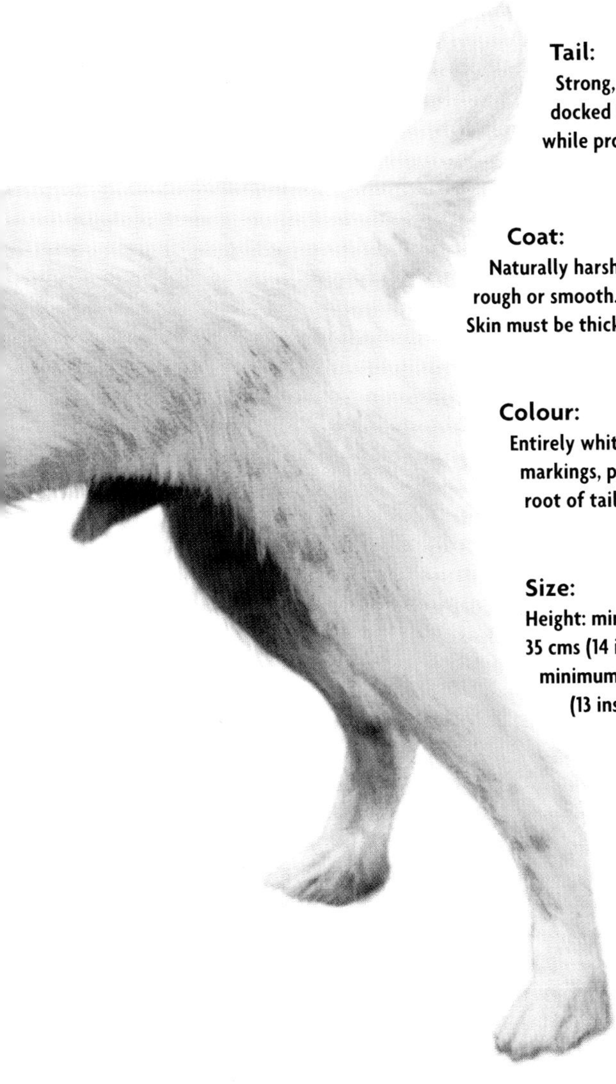

**Tail:**
Strong, straight, set on high. Customarily docked with length complimenting the body while providing a good handhold.

**Coat:**
Naturally harsh, close and dense, whether rough or smooth. Belly and undersides coated. Skin must be thick and loose.

**Colour:**
Entirely white or with tan, lemon or black markings, preferably confined to head or root of tail.

**Size:**
Height: minimum 33 cms (13 ins), ideally 35 cms (14 ins) at withers for dogs, and minimum 30 cms (12 ins), ideally 33 cms (13 ins) at withers for bitches.

**Feet:**
Compact with firm pads, turning neither in nor out.

# Jack and Parson Russell Terriers

*by Christina Pettersall*

# Table of Contents

**9**

**History of the**
Parson Jack Russell Terrier

Intelligent, energetic and agile, the Jack Russell is a terrier in every sense of the word and one of the world's most popular breeds. Learn about 'Father of the Breed' Parson John Russell and the evolution of the game, hard-working dogs that bear his name.

**18**

**Charateristics of the**
Parson Jack Russell Terrier

Are you ready for a Jack Russell? Find out about the breed's personality—-energetic, athletic, headstrong yet loving—-and see if you're a suitable Jack Russell owner. Also learn about the breed's physical characteristics and health concerns in the breed.

**25**

**Breed Standard for the**
Parson Jack Russell Terrier

Learn the requirements of a well-bred Jack Russell by studying the description of the breed set forth in The Kennel Club standard. Both show dogs and pets must possess key characteristics as outlined in the breed standard.

**30**

**Your Puppy**
Parson Jack Russell Terrier

Be advised about choosing a reputable breeder and selecting a healthy, typical puppy. Understand the responsibilities of ownership, including home preparation, acclimatization, the vet and prevention of common puppy problems.

**58**

**Everyday Care of Your**
Parson Jack Russell Terrier

Enter into a sensible discussion of dietary and feeding considerations, exercise, grooming, travelling and identification of your dog. This chapter discusses Jack Russell care for all stages of development.

DISTRIBUTED BY:

**INTERPET**
PUBLISHING

Vincent Lane, Dorking
Surrey RH4 3YX
England

ISBN 13: 978 1 902389 39 4
ISBN 10: 1 902389 39 5

*by Charlotte Schwartz*

Be informed about the importance of training your Jack Russell from the basics of housebreaking and understanding the development of a young dog to executing obedience commands (sit, stay, down, etc.).

Experience the dog show world, including different types of shows and the making up of a champion. Go beyond the conformation ring to working trials and agility trials, etc.


PHOTO CREDITS

Photos by Carol Ann Johnson with addtional photos by:

Norvia Behling
TJ Calhoun
Carolina Biological Supply
David Dalton
Doskocil
Isabelle Francais
James Hayden-Yoav
James R Hayden, RBP
Bill Jonas
Alice van Kempen
Dwight R Kuhn
Dr Dennis Kunkel
Mikki Pet Products
Phototake
Jean Claude Revy
Alice Roche
Steven Surfman
Dr Andrew Spielman
Karen Taylor
C James Webb

Illustrations by Renée Low

Recognise the signs of an ageing dog, both behavioural and medical; implement a senior-care programme with your veterinary surgeon and become comfortable with making the final decisions and arrangements for your senior Jack Russell.




Cover design patented: US 6,435,559 B2
Printed in South Korea


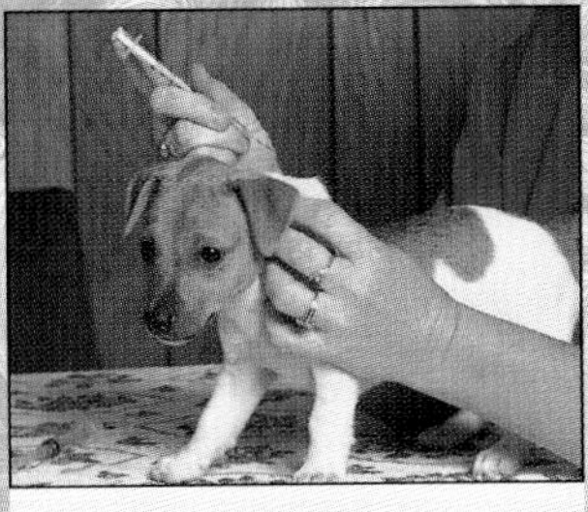



Discover how to select a proper veterinary surgeon and care for your dog at all stages of life. Topics include vaccination scheduling, skin problems, dealing with external and internal parasites and the medical conditions common to the breed.

Learn to recognise and handle common behavioural problems in your Parson Jack Russell Terrier, including barking, jumping up, aggression with people and other dogs, chewing, digging, etc.

DANIEL FROHMAN
PRESENTS
MARY PICKFORD
IN
"RAGS"
PRODUCED BY
FAMOUS PLAYERS FILM CO.
ADOLPH ZUKOR, PRES

The famous silent film star Mary Pickford, starring in a film called RAGS, used a Jack Russell Terrier as her supporting actor. The street name for Miss Pickford in the film was Rags. She came across some bullies maltreating a dog by tying tins onto its body so it would make noise whilst running. Miss Rags chased the bullies and adopted the Jack Russell Terrier—which she named Rags, of course.

HISTORY OF THE

# PARSON JACK RUSSELL TERRIER

The Jack Russell Terrier is a smallish dog, full of vitality, very intelligent, warm and gentle. It makes a charming house pet.

The Parson Jack Russell Terrier is a sensibly built, bright, very energetic dog that has become very popular on both sides of the Atlantic. His roots are from England and the breeder of note in his background was a parson, as colourful and active a figure as the little dog that he championed. This is a game dog, bred for hunting, full of mischievous behaviour and unlimited energy. If you are considering adding a Jack Russell to your household you must be aware of the breed's attributes as well as the problems of owning this breed.

This book will give you the history, description and standard of the Jack Russell. You will also learn about puppy care, training and the health of the breed. With the colour photos you will see how alert, bright and scrappy this plucky little dog can be.

All terriers are active, busy dogs and the Jack Russell is even more so. However, if you like a lively, challenging dog and are ready to make a commitment to training, this may be the dog for you. And, as is true with most breeds, once you give your heart to a Jack Russell you will remain a devotee to the breed for a lifetime.

**Did You Know?**

At the Jack Russell Inn near Barnstaple, Devon, you will see the inn's sign with a reproduction of Trump, taken from a portrait that the Reverend Russell had painted of his favourite dog during her lifetime.

**ORIGIN OF THE BREED**

The Parson Jack Russell Terrier belongs to the group of dogs described as terriers, from the Latin word *terra*, meaning earth. The terrier is a dog that has been bred to work beneath the ground to drive out small and large vermin, rodents and other animals that can be a nuisance to country living.

All of the dogs in the Terrier Group originated in the British Isles with the exception of the Miniature Schnauzer. Many of the terrier breeds were derived from a similar ancestor and, as recently as the mid-1800s, the terriers fell roughly into two basic categories: the rough-coated, short-legged dogs, which tended to come from Scotland, and the longer legged, smooth-coated dogs, which were bred in England. The terriers, although they may differ in type, all have the same character, being game dogs that go after vermin and that also make good companions for their masters.

The terrier background is obscure but what was certain is that in the 1700s and early 1800s there was no definite breed of terrier, but that the dogs were bred to go to ground with courage and conviction. Those who were unable to do the job were destroyed and those who could do the proper work were bred to one another with little regard for type. 'Unless they were fit and game for the purpose, their heads were not kept long out of the huge butt of water in the stable yard.' Those who bred and kept dogs had a specific purpose of work for their particular breed. They bred long legs for speed, short legs for going to ground, double coat for protection against the elements and, common to all terriers, a powerful set of teeth.

As early as 1735, the *Sportsman's Dictionary* described the terrier as 'as a kind of hound, used only or chiefly for hunting the fox or badger. He creeps into the ground and then nips and bites the fox and badger, either by tearing them in pieces with his teeth, or else hauling them and pulling them by force out of their lurking holes.' In 1845 Youatt wrote under the heading of *Terriers*, 'The ears of moderate size, half erect, usually of a deep black colour with a yellow spot over the eye...The coat of the

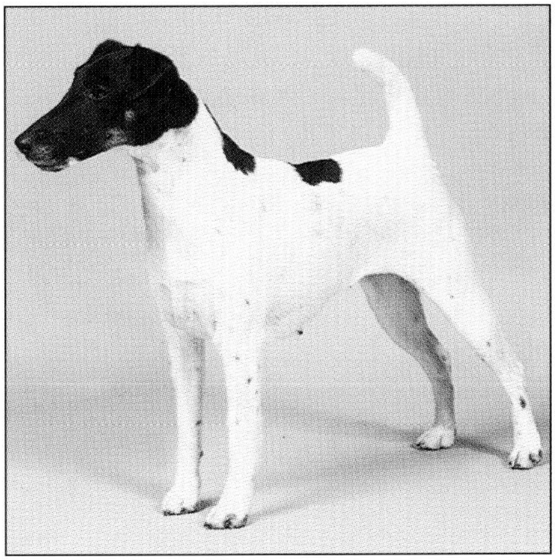

**The legs of a Jack Russell provide both speed for running and strength for digging.**

Terrier may be either smooth or rough...the rough terrier possibly obtained his shaggy coat from the cur, and the smooth terrier may derive from the hound.' James Watson in *The Dog Book* wrote, 'The summing up of the situation is that the terrier was developed from the common material of England. A hard-biting, game dog, small enough to go to earth after the fox and badger.'

John (Jack) Russell, the 'father' of the breed, was born in 1795 in Dartmouth and grew up in North Devon. His father was a sportsman with a great interest in the hounds, the terriers and the hunt. In addition, the senior Russell was also a highly regarded reverend. His son grew up with the dogs and from a very young age had a keen interest in animals and in hunting. While at Oxford, he noticed a smart little Fox Terrier on the local milk wagon and promptly purchased the bitch. Named Trump, she was said to be 'Neat as a pin, her lines were splendid, her form absolutely balanced, her outlook keen and stylish.' Nearly completely white,

**Opposite page: This six month-old bitch Parson Jack Russell Terrier says it all with her kindly, intelligent eyes that say 'Come, play with me!'**

**A Smooth Fox Terrier served as the basis of the new breed created by Parson Jack Russell.**

**The Miniature Wire-Haired Dachshund may have been used to shorten the leg length of early Jack Russells and to improve their ability to dig.**

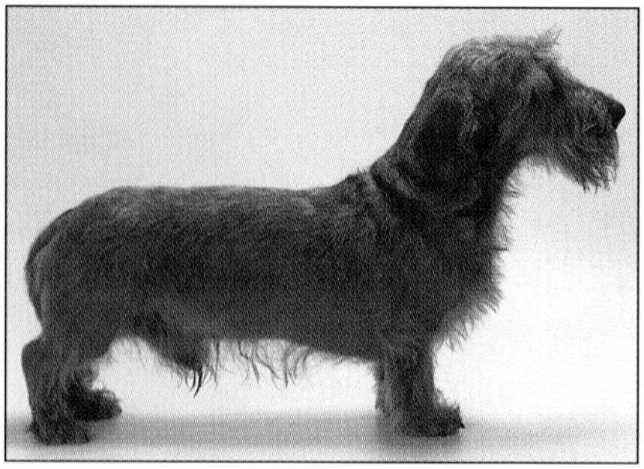

she had a thick, dense coat, which gave her not only ample protection against the inclement weather but also protection against injury from the brambles and underbrush as she was pursuing the fox. She became the foundation of the breed and it was said that she was in the background of every Jack Russell born during the next 50 years.

Russell was ordained a minister in 1819. He was an ardent preacher and apparently well liked as he made the rounds of the neighbouring pulpits when asked to preach. He was noted for his kindness (he never sold a dog, only gave them away) and for his love of animals.

The Jack Russell, unlike the other terriers, was, has been and still is bred primarily as a hunting dog and not bred for the show ring. Of primary concern has been the breed's ability to go to ground and to bolt the foxes for the hounds and the hunters. This is a tough, working breed that is expected to and wants to put in a day's work in the field.

Jack Russell was a well-known foxhunter and his terriers were known throughout the country. He preferred dogs that would run with the hounds and that could tease and worry the fox until the hunters arrived. He did not want dogs that would kill the fox, thus ending the chase, but wanted intelligent dogs that would do a day's work with courage and conviction.

In addition to Russell's bitch Trump, three other dogs were pillars of the early breed. They were Old Trap, Old Jock and Grove Nettle. All three dogs are prominent in the background of the Fox Terrier.

Old Trap, sired by Tip, another well-known dog, weighed 17 pounds and was renowned for his gameness and terrier character. He was used extensively for stud and founded the Old Trap line that excelled in strength of jaw and expression. Old Jock was born in 1859 and had good bone, straight legs and excellent feet. He

### Did You Know?

The Jack Russell Terrier Club of America is the largest Jack Russell club and has the largest registry in the world. Membership comes from North America, Great Britain, Australia, South Africa, Sweden, Japan and the Bahamas.

The Pembroke Welsh Corgi, among other breeds, was sometimes used in earlier Jack Russell crosses.

had tan on his ears and black at the root of his tail. He weighed 18 pounds, was somewhat thick in the skull and had plenty of jaw power. Bred by the Huntsman for the Grove, he was the foundation from which many working and show dogs came down. Grove Nettle, whelped in 1862, was a pretty bitch with a profuse coat. She was the first of the wire coats, and could work as well as being good looking. She was a prolific dam and was bred to nearly all the good dogs of her day.

Russell became a founding member of The Kennel Club in 1873 and judged the Fox Terriers at the Crystal Palace show in 1874. It was now obvious that there was a split between the show-type Fox Terrier and the working terriers that Russell preferred. He noted after judging that 'I seldom or never see a real Fox Terrier nowadays!'

Russell's strain of dogs was well respected and Hugh Dalziel in *British Dogs* credited him with being the Father of Fox Terrier breeders. The parson died in 1883 and the Kennel Club *Gazette* noted that 'as the oldest Fox Terrier breeder in England, Mr Russell's connection with The Kennel Club was an honour to that body.'

About 1895 the Parson Jack Russell Terrier Club was founded and one of their aims was to 'encourage the breeding of the old-fashioned North Devon Fox Terrier, brought to prominence particularly through the terriers bred by the Reverend John Russell.'

Arthur Heinemann became

## Did You Know?

Mona Huxham, author and breeder of Jack Russells, attended the centenary festivities of the Reverend Jack Russell in England in April 1983. The centenary committee had amassed a variety of memorabilia such as Russell's silver hunting horns and his library of books, including all of his hunting books. In addition, his hunting top hat and boots were on display. The church records and registry showed 50 years of his presiding over weekly weddings, baptisms and funeral services. In a place of honour was a portrait of his wife, seated on her horse and wearing her hunting dress.

**The Wire Fox Terrier was used early on to create the wire-haired variety of Parson Jack Russell Terrier.**

the secretary of this organisation and he continued where the parson had left off, becoming a great promoter and breeder of the Jack Russell. Heinemann bought as many terriers as he could locate whose lines traced directly back to the parson's dogs. In 1909 Mr Heinemann judged the Working Fox Terriers at Crufts, classes that were given to encourage the breeding of the type of dog that the Reverend Russell had bred.

By 1900 the Fox Terrier was a prominent class at the dog shows and the entries were refined and elegant. However, the little Jack Russell continued to be very popular as a working dog. In Devon and Somerset in particular the old strains of Russell's terrier were carefully guarded and the puppies were usually sold only to those who would be working the dogs.

By 1925 Arthur Heinemann argued in a court of law that the Jack Russell Terrier was a distinct breed and had been pure-bred for many generations, and, although not recognised by The Kennel Club, the terriers had considerable value. The judge agreed.

Breeders who were active in the breed in Great Britain in the 1920s and 1930s were Augusta Guest of the Inwood Kennels, who had several of Heinemann's dogs; Lord Coventry, Master of the Carmanthenshire Hounds, who often bred back to Heinemann's dogs; and W. Thornton of the Workwell Kennels who had bred the breed for nearly 70 years. Later, Vernon Bartlett, Sid Churchill and Bernard Tuck continued to breed the old-fashioned working dog.

After World War II there were few pure-bred Jack Russells around. A breeder would take a low-legged Fox Terrier and cross it with a Dachshund or a Corgi. Others would cross their dogs with Sealyhams. By now, the breed was a very diverse lot, not

## Did You Know?

Jack Horner wrote in *Terriers of the World*, 'A prominent breeder in those days was the Rev. John Russell whose strain excelled in their work but were not exhibited.' Russell is reported not to have minded if a terrier had one short leg and three long ones, provided it was up to the work required of it.

only in length of body but in size, ear carriage and coat texture.

A variety of Jack Russell clubs, each pushing its own type of dog, sprang up. The first of these clubs, established in the late 1890s, was the Parson Jack Russell Terrier Club (PJRTC), which was previously called the Devon and Somerset Badger Digging Club. Arthur Heinemann served as secretary of this group for many years. Its purpose was to encourage the breeding of the old-fashioned North Devon Fox Terrier. Badger digging was one of the main activities of this organisation. Eventually this club died out.

By 1975, the Jack Russell Terrier Club of Great Britain (JRTCGB) was formed. In 1978 the South Eastern Jack Russell Club was formed as a breakaway group from the JRTCGB. All of the clubs were beset with the problems of size and type for the Jack Russell. The SEJRC divided the Jack Russell into two sizes, miniature and standard. The terriers owned by the members of this organisation were short legged and longer backed in type than other JRs. The standard described the dog as a 'working terrier' but its members had little interest in working their dogs.

The clubs eventually agreed upon a basic standard with differences in height still remaining. By 1983, the SEJRC formally applied for Kennel Club recognition. By now, the old Parson Jack Russell Terrier Club was revived to safeguard the traditional terrier with Vernon Bartlett serving as president. Their first task was to request recognition by The Kennel Club of the old type terrier that was bred in the 1800s.

The acrimony between the various clubs was great and eventually The Kennel Club was taken aback at the opposition of the SEJRC's requests for recognition. After many letters, phone calls, meetings and negotiations regarding the foundation register and the breed standard, the PJRTC

## Information . . .

**Badger digging consisted of using terriers to locate the badger and to dig it out of its hole. The badger was then 'bagged,' put in a box and weighed and then released. The season was from April**

**through October and the meets were published in the local press. The meet lasted all day with the ladies, at the noon hour, serving sandwiches, bread, cheese, cider and beer.**

was able to announce that the Parson Jack Russell Terrier was officially a breed. In 1997 the Jack Russell Terrier was able to win Challenge Certificates for the first time at a sanctioned show.

## JACK RUSSELLS AROUND THE WORLD

The Jack Russell was exported to Australia as early as the 1880s and included dogs of the Parson Russell's line. Many dogs were imported from England over the years and the Jack Russell Terrier Club of Australia, Inc, formed in 1972, was the first breed club to function since the demise of the PRJTC. This is a large, strong organisation with its own breed registry system. It has registered over 6000 litters since its beginnings. In 1991 the breed received official recognition from the Australian Kennel Club.

It is unknown when the first Jack Russells were imported to the United States, but by 1976 the Jack Russell Terrier Club of America (JRTCA) was formed and there are now close to 3000 members. Their purpose is 'to promote and maintain the Jack Russell as a breed of terrier.' The

**The Jack Russell Terrier is quickly becoming a favourite dog in the USA with thousands of members in the Jack Russell Terrier Club of America. Breed popularity is growing in Australia as well.**

**Parson Jack Russells are athletic dogs who welcome the opportunity to romp together on any terrain.**

Jack Russell Terrier Breeders Association was founded in 1985 and its purpose is to 'promote the Jack Russell Terrier as it was developed in the 1880s by Parson John Russell.' This group offers shows and trials as well as a bi-monthly newsletter and an annual yearbook.

The JRTCA keeps the national registry of the Jack Russell Terrier in America, which is the largest registry in the world. Entries for their national trial can exceed 1000 including JR's from throughout North America. They publish a bi-monthly magazine, *True Grit*, and an annual two-volume yearbook, as well as a breeder directory. In addition, they operate a Jack Russell Terrier Rescue service that assists in retraining and finding homes for displaced Jack Russells. They also operate a very informative web site.

In 1999 the Jack Russell was accepted to enter the Miscellaneous Classes at American Kennel Club sanctioned shows.

Jack Russells are popular in the Netherlands and they are very popular in Germany, where there is a JRTC Deutschland and a Working Parson Jack Russell Terrier Club Germany. JRs are found in the Scandinavian countries as well as in South Africa, where over 2000 JRs have been registered.

The little terrier, championed by a parson from North Devon, has come a long way, with his popularity evident throughout the world.

## CHARACTERISTICS OF THE

# PARSON JACK RUSSELL TERRIER

The essentials of the Parson Jack Russell Terrier are well summarised by the descriptions in the various breed standards. The Kennel Club's standard uses the adjectives workmanlike, active, agile, bold and friendly to illustrate the breed's overall temperament and personality. The American Kennel Club's standard for the Jack Russell Terrier states, 'The terrier must present a lively, active and alert appearance. It should impress with its fearless and happy disposition. It should be remembered that the Jack Russell is a working terrier and should retain these instincts. Nervousness, cowardice or over-aggressiveness should be discouraged and it should always appear confident.' All over the world, the Jack Russell is known for being an active and confident breed, and the retention of his working instincts are constantly emphasised.

Please consider these descriptions of the breed very carefully if you are planning on adding a Jack Russell to your family. Note especially the adjectives that are commonly associated with the breed: lively, active, alert, fearless, confident.

Of all the terrier breeds, the Jack Russell is the one who has stayed the closest to the purpose for which he was bred—to hunt, to chase the fox and to dig the badger out of his hole. He has a love of fields and open spaces and

**Jack Russells abound with energy and life. They can run, play and chase for hours on end.**

he can run all day keeping up with the hounds. He is a strong and healthy dog and he does not like to be confined. He is hardy and adaptable and 'Quick as Spitfire.'

This is a high-energy dog and one who will take over the household if given half a chance. A strong warning is that he must never be allowed to think he has the upper hand. He must receive consistent and strong leadership by his master. He loves to dig in the yard, loves to go under the fence (harking back to his badger-digging days) and he will have a tendency to roam if not confined to an area. He should not be left alone with birds or rodents but can get along with cats if introduced properly.

Although there are negatives to the breed, there are very positive aspects to owning a Jack Russell. He is a very adaptable dog and one who can change his living circumstances easily. He is very intelligent and very hardy. He makes a loving and happy companion who readily joins into the family fun. He is an excellent companion and works easily and well as a therapy dog. In addition, the Jack Russell is easy to groom and of a nice size.

The Jack Russell can adapt

## Did You Know?

On the JRTCA's *The Bad Dog Talk* web page, the following guidelines for prospective owners are listed:

Jack Russell Terriers—
Require firm and consistent discipline
Require at least basic obedience training
Absolutely need a securely fenced yard

Can be destructive if left unattended and unemployed
Are not recommended as apartment or condo dogs
Will not tolerate abuse from a child
Require a long-term commitment

These are essential points to consider in determining your suitablility as a Parson Jack Russell Terrier owner.

## Information . . .

Jack Russell Terrier owners should have fun with their dogs! Not only will they thrive in organised activities but they love being part of the family, going for rides in the car, fetching a ball (sometimes for hours on end, to his owner's dismay), helping in the kitchen by keeping the floor clean and then cuddling up for a snooze on the bed when day is done.

from being a hunting dog to being a well-behaved housedog, but he must be trained consistently to behave like a gentleman. A long-time breeder wrote, 'If he is an intelligent dog and mostly a very loving one too, and if the brains he needs to do his work well are harnessed to his affection for his master or mistress and if the whole training business can be carried out as a game with endless patience expended by the owner and lots of praise meted out to him, the result will be of the greatest benefit to everyone.'

Puppies must be well socialised and this is an important factor when selecting the breeder of your Jack Russell. Aggressive behaviour toward other dogs or people must not be tolerated. Do not be fooled by the Jack Russell that you see on television or in the movies.

Obedience with your Jack Russell should be a consideration, as well it should be for many breeds of dogs. Six sessions of obedience will at least teach you and your dog the rudiments of stay, come, sit and heel. All terriers can be a challenge in the obedience ring. Terriers are not easy to work with in obedience, as their intelligence and independent spirit can sometimes make them more trying to train than had been anticipated. You will see Golden Retrievers, Poodles and Miniature Schnauzers in

Jack Russells get along well with other dogs if they are properly socialised.

Jack Russells are eager to learn all kinds of tricks. They are highly agile and have great balance.

abundance in obedience classes, as these are breeds that are easy to work with. Not only are they intelligent, but more importantly, they have a willingness to please their masters.

The Jack Russell is easily distracted and busy, but he is an intelligent dog and he does respond to training. Of course, when training a smart and independent dog, the handler will often learn humility whilst the dog is learning his sits and stays.

If you are an active individual, which you should be if you own a Jack Russell, agility trials may be just the ticket for you and your dog. Jack Russells have been very successful in this area.

The Jack Russell is a very healthy dog. All terriers in general are healthy, but nearly all breeds have one or more genetic problems. On the contrary, the Jack Russell has few hereditary problems. On occasion lens luxation and cataracts will appear in some lines, and patellar luxation (slipped knee caps) will appear in other lines. Be sure to enquire of your breeder if she has any hereditary problems that show up in her dogs.

You should give your dog a clean area for sleeping, feed him a

## Did You Know?

Jack Russell Terrier clubs will offer working trials and match shows for the breed and oftentimes will draw large entries. These are often full-day events filled with fun, including trials, food, companionship and all types of activities to keep the entire family busy and happy.

They may seem inexhaustible, but Jack Russells enjoy quiet time at home, too.

reputable dog food and give him plenty of fresh water. If your Jack Russell is active all day, every day, you will probably want to feed him more than the suggested feeding schedule that comes with the dog food, as he will be burning up many calories in his active life. Take him for his daily runs and be sure to take care of any wounds he may receive. Take him to the veterinary surgeon for his yearly check-up and shots. You may want to have a stool sample checked periodically if you suspect he may have worms. Do not let your Jack Russell run loose with the chance he may be hit by a car and watch him around the swimming pools so that he does not fall in and, unable to get out, drown. Follow this advice and your Jack Russell Terrier should live to be twelve to fourteen years old.

## Did You Know?

Do you want to live longer? If you like to volunteer, it is wonderful if you can take your well-behaved Jack Russell to a nursing home once a week for several hours. The elder community loves to have a dog to visit with and often your dog will bring a bit of companionship to someone who is either lonely or who may be somewhat detached from the world. You will not only be bringing happiness to someone else, but you will be keeping your little dog busy—and we haven't even mentioned the fact that it has been discovered that volunteering helps to increase your longevity!

**Although your Parson Jack Russell may love to romp through fields, allowing her to run loose is dangerous. In her enthusiasm she may not see an on-coming car or lorry.**

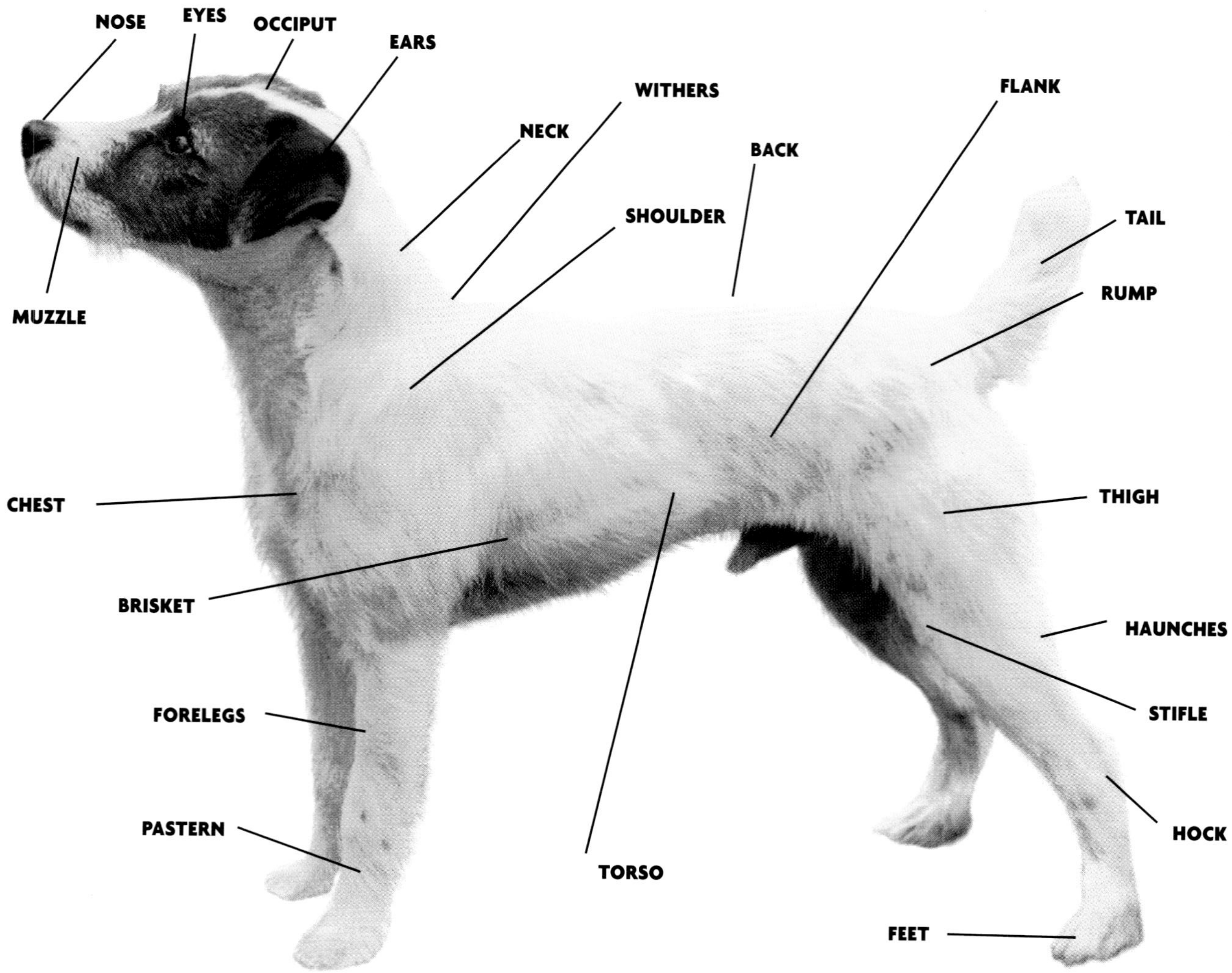
NOSE
EYES
OCCIPUT
EARS
WITHERS
FLANK
NECK
BACK
SHOULDER
TAIL
RUMP
MUZZLE
CHEST
THIGH
BRISKET
HAUNCHES
FORELEGS
STIFLE
PASTERN
HOCK
TORSO
FEET

# BREED STANDARD FOR THE PARSON JACK RUSSELL TERRIER

Each breed approved by The Kennel Club has a standard that gives the reader and the judge a mental picture of what the specific breed should look like. All reputable breeders strive to produce animals that will meet the requirements of the standard. Many breeds were developed for a specific purpose, i.e. hunting, retrieving, going to ground, coursing, guarding, herding, or for working. The terriers, and certainly including the Parson Jack Russell Terrier, were bred to go to ground and to pursue vermin. In addition to having dogs that *look* like proper Jack Russells, the standard assures that the Jack Russell will have the personality, disposition and intelligence that are sought in the breed.

Standards were originally written by fanciers who had a love and a concern for the breed. They knew that the essential characteristics of the Jack Russell were unlike any other breed and that care must be taken that these characteristics—physical, personality and working ability—were maintained through the generations.

As time progressed, breeders became more aware that certain areas of the dog needed a better description or more definition. In order to modify the standard, the national club will select five or more breeders to meet together and work changes into the standard. However, standards for any breed are never changed on a whim and serious study and exchange between breeders takes place before any move is made.

**The breed standard is crucial to the dog show judging process and helps assure that the offspring of purebred dogs look like their parents, more or less. Dog show judges measure the dogs against the standard and select the dog that most closely matches it. There is no such thing as a perfect dog.**

**THE KENNEL CLUB'S BREED STANDARD FOR THE PARSON JACK RUSSELL TERRIER (INTERIM)**

**General Appearance:** Workmanlike, active and agile; built for speed and endurance.

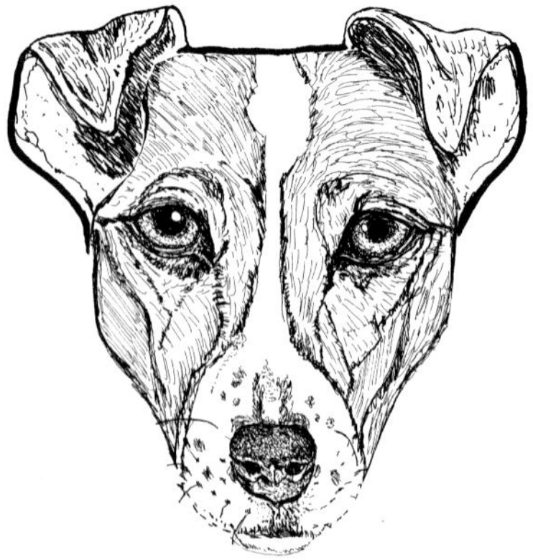

Correct ears.

**Characteristics:** Essentially a working terrier with ability and conformation to go to ground and run with hounds.

**Temperament:** Bold and friendly.

**Head and Skull:** Flat, moderately broad, gradually narrowing to the eyes. Shallow stop. Length from nose to stop slightly shorter than from stop to occiput. Nose black.

Bad ears; the fold is atop the skull.

**Eyes:** Almond-shaped, fairly deep-set, dark, keen expression.

**Mouth:** Jaws strong, muscular. Teeth with a perfect, regular and complete scissor bite, i.e. upper teeth closely overlapping lower teeth and set square to the jaws.

**Neck:** Clean, muscular, of good length, gradually widening to shoulder.

**Forequarters:** Shoulders long and sloping, well laid back, cleanly cut at withers. Legs strong, must be straight with joints turning neither in nor out. Elbows close to body, working free of the sides.

**Body:** Chest of moderate depth, capable of being spanned behind the shoulders by average size hands. Back strong and straight. Loin slightly arched. Well balanced, length of back from withers to root of tail equal to height from withers to ground.

**Feet:** Compact with firm pads, turning neither in nor out.

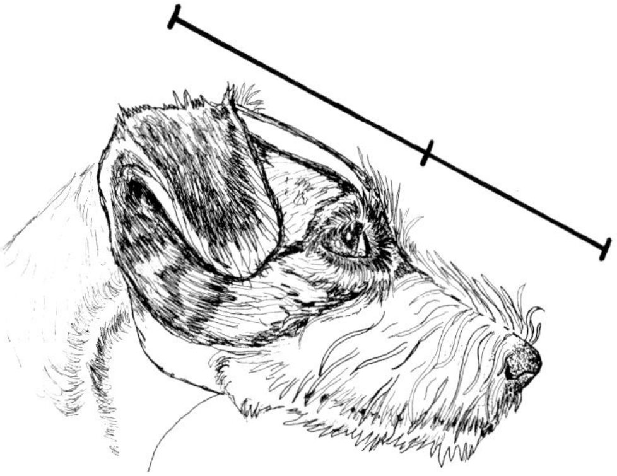

Correct muzzle.

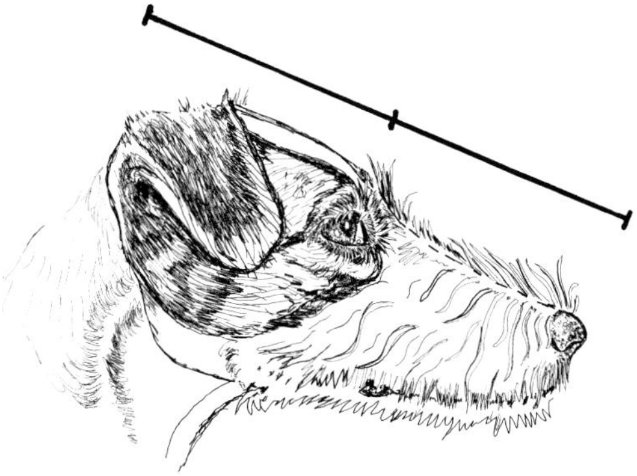

Bad muzzle; too long.

**Tail:** Strong, straight, set on high. Customarily docked with length complimenting the body while providing a good handhold.

**Gait/Movement:** Free, lively, well co-ordinated; straight action front and behind.

**Coat:** Naturally harsh, close and dense, whether rough or smooth. Belly and undersides coated. Skin must be thick and loose.

**Colour:** Entirely white or with tan, lemon or black markings, preferably confined to head or root of tail.

**Size:** Height: minimum 33 cms (13 ins), ideally 35 cms (14 ins) at withers for dogs, and minimum 30 cms (12 ins), ideally 33 cms (13 ins) at withers for bitches.

**Faults:** Any departure from the foregoing points should be considered a fault and the seriousness with which the fault should be regarded should be in exact proportion to its degree.

**Note:** Male animals should have two apparently normal testicles fully descended into the scrotum.

## Did You Know?

In contrast to The Kennel Club's standard, which is quite specific in its height range for both dogs and bitches, the American Kennel Club's standard calls for the Jack Russell to measure between 10 and 15 inches at the withers. For a relatively small dog, the five-inch difference is quite a wide range. Dogs who are only 10 inches at the withers will usually be low set with a longer body and those who are 15 inches at the withers will be higher on leg and likely to have a shorter body.

**Rough coat.**

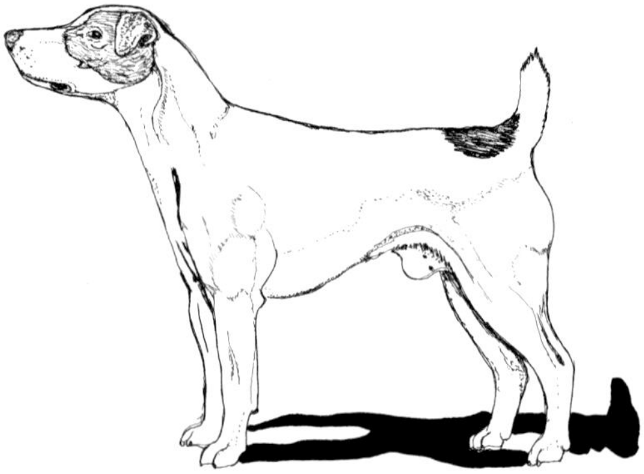

**Smooth coat.**

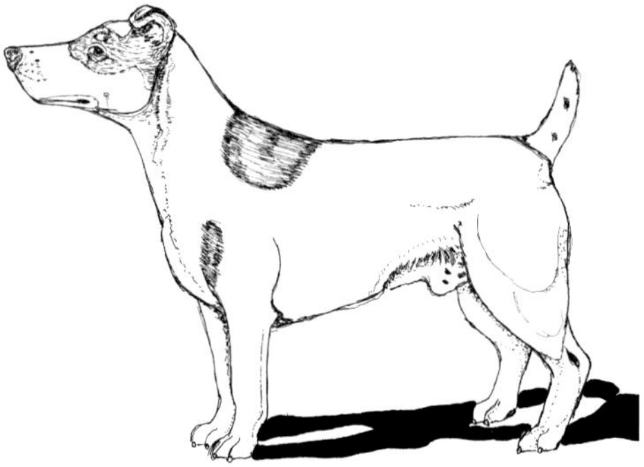

**Legs too short.**

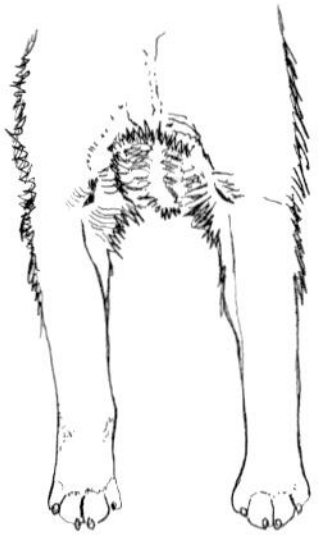

**Correct front.**

**Incorrect; toes out.**

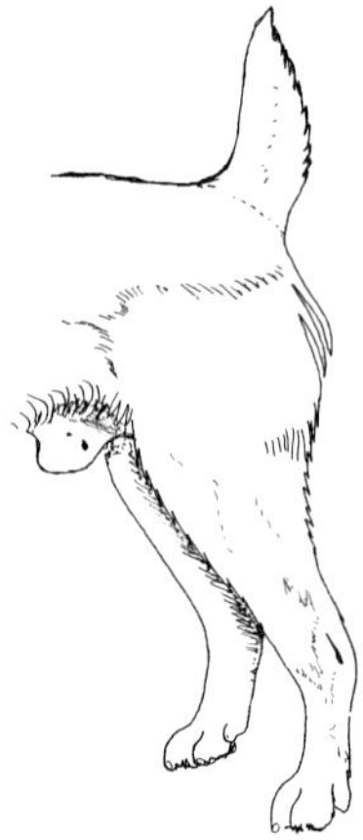

**Correct tail.**

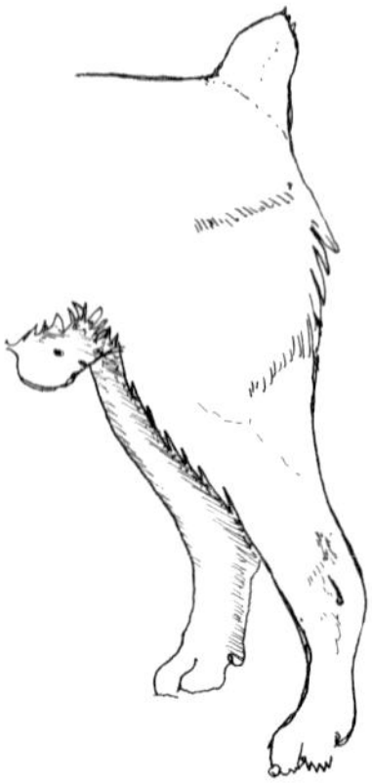

**Tail too short.**

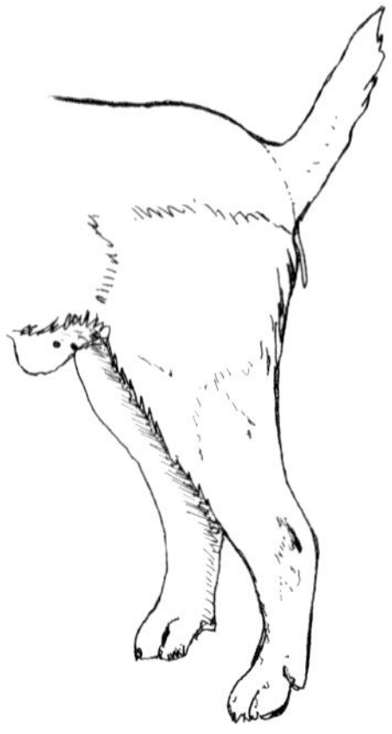

**Bad tail; too low set.**

Top left: Old-fashioned male with short legs. Top right: An old-fashioned bitch with legs too short for modern standards. Bottom: Compare this modern Parson Jack Russell Terrier with the two dogs shown above. Note the radical difference in leg length.

# PARSON JACK RUSSELL TERRIER

### WHERE TO BEGIN?

If you are convinced that the Parson Jack Russell Terrier is the ideal dog for you, it's time to learn about where to find a puppy and what to look for. Locating a litter of Jack Russells should not present a problem for the new owner. You should inquire about breeders in your area who enjoy a good reputation in the breed. You are looking for an established breeder with outstanding dog ethics and a strong commitment to the breed. New owners should have as many questions as they have doubts. An established breeder is indeed the one to answer your four million questions and make you comfortable with your choice of the Jack Russell. An established breeder will sell you a puppy at a fair price if, and only if, the breeder determines that you are a suitable, worthy owner of his/her dogs. An established breeder can be relied upon for advice, no matter what time of day or night. A reputable breeder will accept a puppy back, without questions, should you decide that this is not the right dog for you.

**When selecting your Parson Jack Russell puppy, select one who is alert and friendly. Any of these puppies would qualify!**

When choosing a breeder, reputation is much more important than convenience of location. Do not be overly impressed by breeders who run brag advertisements in the presses about their stupendous champions and working lines. The real quality breeders are quiet and unassuming. You hear about them at the dog trials and shows, by word of mouth. You may be well advised to avoid

## Did You Know?

Unfortunately, when a puppy is bought by someone who does not take into consideration the time and attention that dog ownership requires, it is the puppy who suffers when he is either abandoned or placed in a shelter by a frustrated owner. So all of the 'homework' you do in preparation for your pup's arrival will benefit you both. The more informed you are, the more

you will know what to expect and the better equipped you will be to handle the ups and downs of raising a puppy. Hopefully, everyone in the household is willing to do his part in raising and caring for the pup. The anticipation of owning a dog often brings a lot of promises from excited family members: 'I will walk him every day,' 'I will feed him,' 'I will housebreak him,' etc., but these things take time and effort, and promises can easily be forgotten once the novelty of the new pet has worn off.

the novice who lives only a couple miles away. The local novice breeder, trying so hard to get rid of that first litter of puppies, is more than accommodating and anxious to sell you one. That breeder will charge you as much as any established breeder. The novice breeder isn't going to interrogate you and your family about your intentions with the puppy, the environment and training you can provide, etc. That breeder will be nowhere to be found when your poorly bred, badly adjusted four-pawed monster starts to growl and spit up at midnight or eat the family cat!

Whilst health considerations in the Jack Russell are not nearly as daunting as in most other breeds, socialisation is a breeder concern of immense importance. Since the Jack Russell's temperament can vary from line to line, socialisation is the first and best way to encourage a proper, stable personality.

Choosing a breeder is an important first step in dog ownership. Fortunately, the majority of Jack Russell breeders are devoted to the breed and its well-being. New owners should have little problem finding a reputable breeder who doesn't live on the other side of the country (or in

**Select a breeder who can help you find the right puppy. Usually the most outgoing and friendly puppies are sold first.**

a different country). The Kennel Club is able to recommend breeders of quality Jack Russells, as can any local all-breed club or Jack Russell club. Potential owners are encouraged to attend hunts to see the Jack Russells in action, to meet the owners and handlers firsthand and to get an idea of what Jack Russells look like outside a photographer's lens. Provided you approach the handlers when they are not terribly busy with the dogs, most are more than willing to answer questions, recommend breeders and give advice.

Now that you have contacted and met a breeder or two and made your choice about which breeder is best suited to your needs, it's time to visit the litter. Keep in mind that many top breeders have waiting lists. Sometimes new owners have to wait as long as two years for a puppy. If you are really committed to the breeder whom you've selected, then you will wait (and hope for an early arrival!). If not, you may have to resort to your second or third choice breeder. Don't be too anxious, however. If the breeder doesn't have any waiting list, or any customers, there is probably a good reason. It's no different than visiting a pub with no clientele. The better pubs and restaurants always have a waiting list—and it's usually worth the wait. Besides, isn't a puppy more important than a pint?

Since you are likely

## Did You Know?

You should not even think about buying a puppy that looks sick, undernourished, overly frightened or nervous. Sometimes a

timid puppy will warm up to you after a 30-minute 'let's-get-acquainted' session.

choosing a Jack Russell as a pet dog and not a working dog, you simply should select a pup that is friendly and attractive. Jack Russells generally have fairly large litters, averaging eight puppies, so selection is good once you have located a desirable litter. While the basic structure of the breed has litter variation, the temperament may present trouble in certain strains. Beware of the shy or overly aggressive puppy; be especially conscious of the nervous Jack Russell pup. Don't let sentiment or emotion trap you into buying the runt of the litter.

If you have intentions of your new charge participating in a hunt, consider going to a breeder whose dogs are generally used for that purpose.

The gender of your puppy is largely a matter of personal taste, although there is a common belief amongst those who work with Jack Russells that bitches are quicker to learn and generally more loving and faithful. Males learn more slowly but retain the lesson longer. The difference in size is noticeable but slight. Coloration is not a

**Handle the puppies before you make a decision about which is the puppy best suited for you! Even at a tender age the puppies have interesting personality differences.**

## Information . . .

**Your puppy should have a well-fed appearance but not a distended abdomen, which may indicate worms or incorrect feeding, or both. The body should be firm, with a solid feel. The skin of the abdomen should be pale pink and clean, without signs of scratching or rash. Check the hind legs to make certain that dewclaws were removed, if any were present at birth.**

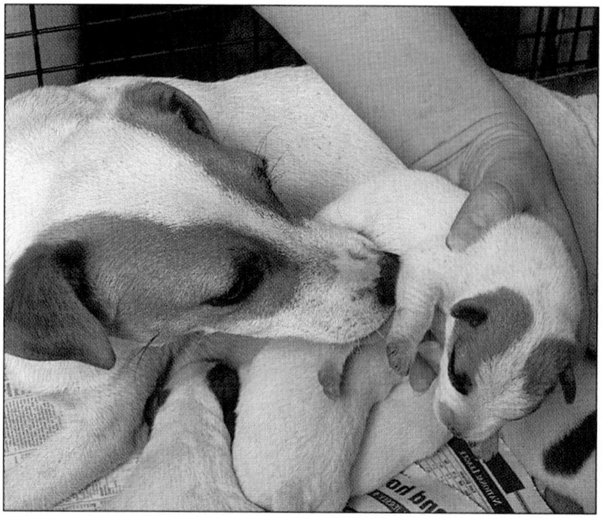

Motherly love is evident bwtween this Jack Russell mum and her pup.

grave concern with this breed.

Breeders commonly allow visitors to see the litter by around the fifth or sixth week, and puppies leave for their new homes between the eighth and tenth week. Breeders who permit their puppies to leave early are more interested in your pounds than their puppies' well-being. Puppies need to learn the rules of the trade from their dams, and most dams continue teaching the pups manners and dos and don'ts until around the eighth week. Breeders spend significant amounts of time with the Jack Russell toddlers so that they are able to interact with the 'other species', i.e. humans. Given the long history that dogs and humans have, bonding between the two species is natural but must be nurtured. A well-bred, well-socialised Jack Russell pup wants nothing more than to be near you and please you.

Always check the bite of your selected puppy to be sure that it is neither overshot nor undershot. This may not be too noticeable on a young puppy but it is always important to check for overall soundness.

## Documentation

Two important documents you will get from the breeder are the pup's pedigree and registration papers. The breeder should register the litter and each pup with The Kennel Club, and it is necessary for you to have the paperwork if you plan on showing or breeding in the future.

Make sure you know the breeder's intentions on which type of registration he will obtain for the pup. There are limited registrations which may prohibit the dog from being shown or from competing in non-conformation trials such as Working or Agility if the breeder feels that the pup is not of sufficient quality to do so. There is also a type of registration that will permit the dog in non-conformation competition only.

## COMMITMENT OF OWNERSHIP

After considering all of these factors, you have most likely already made some very important decisions about selecting your puppy. You have chosen a Jack Russell, which means that you have decided which characteristics you want in a dog and what type of dog will best fit into your family and lifestyle. If you have selected a breeder, you have gone a step further—you have done your research and found a responsible, conscientious person who breeds quality Jack Russells and who should be a reliable source of help as you and your puppy adjust to life together. If you have observed a litter in action, you have obtained a firsthand look at the dynamics of a puppy 'pack' and, thus, you should learn about each pup's individual personality—perhaps you have even found one that particularly appeals to you.

However, even if you have not yet found the Jack Russell puppy of your dreams, observing pups will help you learn to recognise certain behaviour and to determine what a pup's behaviour indicates about his tempera-ment. You will be able to pick out which pups are the leaders,

### Insurance . . .

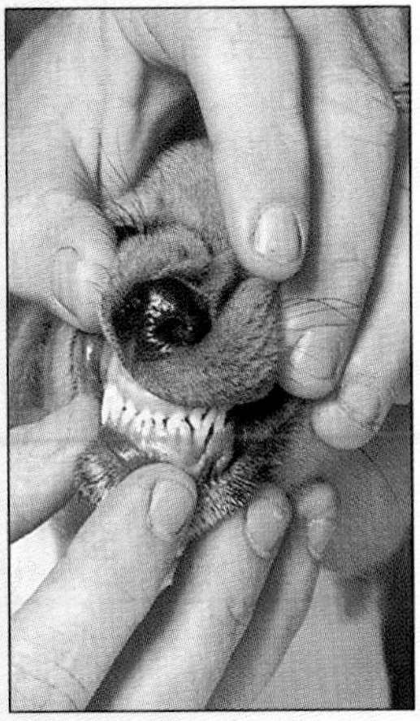

Many good breeders will offer you insurance with your new puppy, which is an excellent idea. The first few weeks of insurance will probably be covered free of charge or with only minimal cost, allowing you to take up the policy when this expires. If you own a pet dog, it is sensible to take out such a policy as veteri-nary fees can be high, although routine vaccinations and boosters are not covered. Look carefully at the many options open to you before deciding which suits you best.

**Owning an active dog like the Jack Russell requires commitment to both training and exercising the dog properly.**

## Information. . .

**Breeders rarely release puppies until they are eight to ten weeks of age. This is an acceptable age for most breeds of dog, excepting toy breeds, which are not released until around 12 weeks, given their petite sizes. If a breeder has a puppy that is 12 weeks or more, it is likely well socialised and housetrained. Be sure that it is otherwise healthy before deciding to take it home.**

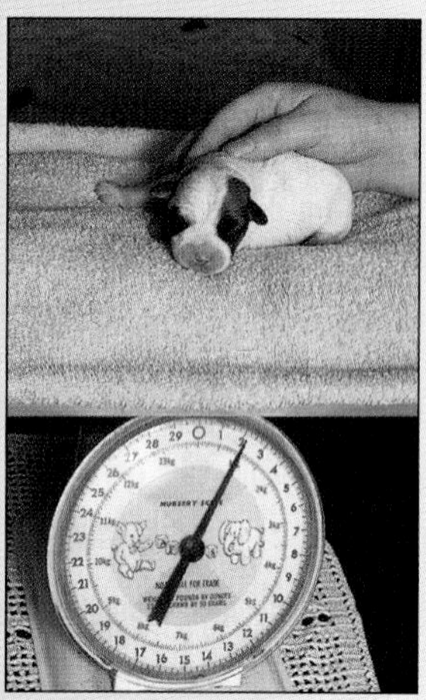

which ones are less outgoing, which ones are confident, which ones are shy, playful, friendly, aggressive, etc. Equally as important, you will learn to recognise what a healthy pup should look and act like. All of these things will help you in your search, and when you find the Jack Russell that was meant for you, you will know it!

Researching your breed, selecting a responsible breeder and observing as many pups as possible are all important steps on the way to dog ownership. It may seem like a lot of effort...and you have not even brought the pup home yet! Remember, though, you cannot be too careful when it comes to deciding on the type of dog you want and finding out about your prospective pup's background. Buying a puppy is not—or should not be—just another whimsical purchase. This is one instance in which you actually do get to choose your own family! You may be thinking that buying a puppy should be fun—it should not be so serious and so much work. Keep in mind that your puppy is not a cuddly stuffed toy or decorative lawn ornament, but a creature that will become a real member of your family. You will come to realise that, whilst buying a puppy is a pleasurable and exciting endeavour, it is not something to be taken lightly. Relax...the fun will start when the pup comes home!

Always keep in mind that a puppy is nothing more than a baby in a furry disguise...a baby who is virtually helpless in a human world and who trusts his owner for fulfilment of his

## Are You a Fit Owner?

If the breeder from whom you are buying a puppy asks you a lot of personal questions, do not be insulted. Such a breeder wants to be sure that you will be a fit provider for his puppy.

basic needs for survival. In addition to water and shelter, your pup needs care, protection, guidance and love. If you are not prepared to commit to this, then you are not prepared to own a dog.

Wait a minute, you say. How hard could this be? All of my neighbours own dogs and they seem to be doing just fine. Why should I have to worry about all of this? Well, you should not worry about it; in fact, you will probably find that once your Jack Russell pup gets used to his new home, he will fall into his place in the family quite naturally. But it never hurts to emphasise the commitment of dog ownership. With some time and patience, it is really not too difficult to raise a curious and exuberant Jack Russell pup to be a well-adjusted and well-mannered adult dog—a dog that could be your most loyal friend.

## Your Schedule . . .

**If you lead an erratic, unpredictable life, with daily or weekly changes in your work requirements, consider the problems of owning a puppy. The new puppy has to be fed regularly, socialised (loved, petted, handled, introduced to other people) and, most importantly, allowed to visit outdoors for toilet training. As the dog gets older, it can be more tolerant of deviations in its feeding and toilet relief.**

### PREPARING PUPPY'S PLACE IN YOUR HOME

Researching your breed and finding a breeder are only two aspects of the 'homework' you will have to do before bringing your Jack Russell puppy home. You will also have to prepare your home and family for the new addition. Much as you would prepare a nursery for a new-born baby, you will need to designate a place in your home that will be the puppy's own. How you prepare your home will depend on how much freedom the dog will be allowed. Whatever you decide, you must ensure that he has a place that he can 'call his own.'

When you bring your new puppy into your home, you are bringing him into what will become his home as well. Obviously, you did not buy a puppy so that he could take over your house, but in order for a puppy to grow into a stable, well-adjusted dog, he has to feel comfortable in his surroundings. Remember, he is

Pups grow up amidst the warmth and companionship of their mother and littermates. Adjusting to life in a human 'pack' takes a little time, but most pups make the transition easily.

leaving the warmth and security of his mother and littermates, as well as the familiarity of the only place he has ever known, so it is important to make his transition as easy as possible. By preparing a place in your home for the puppy, you are making him feel as welcome as possible in a strange new place. It should not take him long to get used to it, but the sudden shock of being transplanted is somewhat traumatic for a young pup. Imagine how a small child would feel in the same situation—that is how your puppy must be feeling. It is up to you to reassure him and to let him know, 'Little fellow, you are going to like it here!'

## WHAT YOU SHOULD BUY

### CRATE

To someone unfamiliar with the use of crates in dog training, it may seem like punishment to shut a dog in a crate, but this is not the case at all. Although all breeders do not advocate crate training, more and more breeders and trainers are recommending crates as a preferred tool for pet puppies as well as show puppies. Crates are not cruel—crates have many humane and highly effective uses in dog care and training. For example, crate training is a very popular and very successful housebreaking method, a crate can keep your dog safe during travel and, perhaps most importantly, a crate provides your dog with a place of his own in your home. It serves as a 'doggie bedroom' of sorts—your Jack Russell can curl up in his crate when he wants to sleep or when he just needs a break. Many dogs sleep in their crates overnight. When lined with soft bedding and with a favourite toy placed inside, a crate becomes a cosy pseudo-den for your dog. Like his ancestors, he too will seek out the comfort and retreat of a den—you just happen to be providing him with something a

**NO Chocolate!**

Use treats to bribe your dog into a desired behaviour. Try small pieces of hard cheese or freeze-dried liver. Never offer chocolate as it has toxic qualities for dogs.

little more luxurious than what his early ancestors enjoyed.

As far as purchasing a crate, the type that you buy is up to you. It will most likely be one of the two most popular types: wire or fibreglass. There are advantages and disadvantages to each type. For example, a wire crate is more open, allowing the air to flow through and affording the dog a view of what is going on around him whilst a fibreglass crate is sturdier. Both can double as travel crates, providing protection for the dog. The size of the crate is another thing to consider. Puppies do not stay puppies forever—in fact, sometimes it seems as if they grow right before your eyes. A Yorkie-sized crate may be fine for a very young Jack Russell pup, but it will not do him much good for long! Unless you have the money and the inclination to buy a new crate every time your pup has a growth spurt, it is better to get one that will accommodate your dog both as a pup and at full size. A medium-size crate will be

## Toxic Plants . . .

**Many plants can be toxic to dogs. If you see your dog carrying a piece of vegetation in his mouth, approach him in a quiet, disinterested manner, avoid eye contact, pet him and gradually remove the plant from his mouth. Alternatively, offer him a treat and maybe he'll drop the plant on his own accord. Be sure no toxic plants are growing in your own garden.**

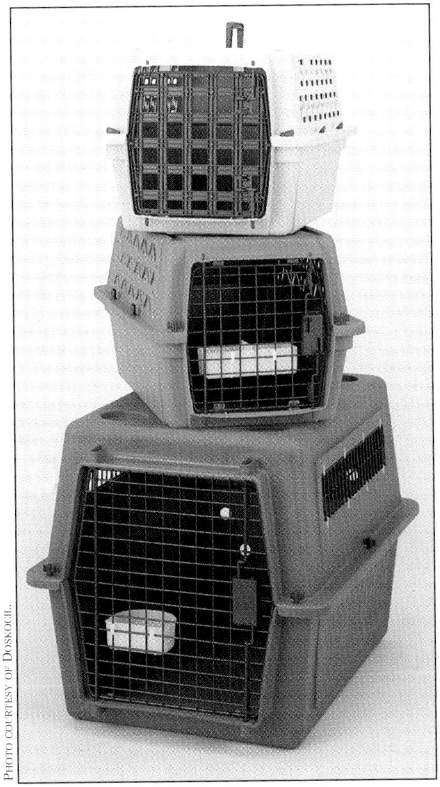

Photo courtesy of Doskocil.

**There are many kinds of crates from which you can select one suitable for your Jack Russell. Your breeder can advise you of the proper sized crate. Obtain a crate large enough for the adult size of your dog.**

A nice, soft bed is always cosy for the Jack Russell puppy, but be alert to his soiling the bedding.

## Crate Training Tips

During crate training, you should partition off the section of the crate in which the pup stays. If he is given too big an area, this will hinder your training efforts. Crate training is based on the fact that a dog does not like to soil his sleeping quarters, so it is ineffective to keep a pup in a crate that is so big that he can eliminate in

one end and get far enough away from it to sleep. Also, you want to make the crate den-like for the pup. Blankets and a favourite toy will make the crate cosy for the small pup; as he grows, you may want to evict some of his 'roommates' to make more room.

It will take some coaxing at first, but be patient. Given some time to get used to it, your pup will adapt to his new home-within-a-home quite nicely.

necessary for a full-grown Jack Russell, who stands approximately 14 inches high.

### Bedding

Veterinary bedding in the dog's crate will help the dog feel more at home and you may also like to pop in a small blanket. This will take the place of the leaves, twigs, etc., that the pup would use in the wild to make a den; the pup can make his own 'burrow' in the crate. Although your pup is far removed from his den-making ancestors, the denning instinct is still a part of his genetic makeup. Second, until you bring your pup home, he has been sleeping amidst the warmth of his mother and littermates, and whilst a blanket is not the same as a warm, breathing body, it still provides heat and something with which to snuggle. You will want to wash your pup's bedding frequently in case he has an accident in his crate, and replace or remove any blanket that becomes ragged and starts to fall apart.

### Toys

Toys are a must for dogs of all ages, especially for curious playful pups. Puppies are the 'children' of the dog world, and what child does not love toys? Chew toys provide enjoyment to both dog and owner—your dog will enjoy playing with his favourite toys, whilst you will enjoy the fact that they distract him from your expensive shoes and leather sofa. Puppies love to chew; in fact, chewing is a

**Early crate training indicates a wise, experienced breeder. This is the kind of person from whom you can confidently acquire a puppy.**

## Toys, Toys, Toys!

**With a big variety of dog toys available, and so many that look like they would be a lot of fun for a dog, be careful in your selection. It is amazing what a set of puppy teeth can do to an innocent-looking toy, so, obviously, safety is a major consideration. Be sure to choose the most durable products that you can find.**

**Hard nylon bones and toys are a safe bet, and many of them are offered in different scents and flavours that will be sure to capture your dog's attention. It is always fun to play a game of catch with your dog, and there are balls and flying discs that are specially made to withstand dog teeth.**

physical need for pups as they are teething, and everything looks appetising! The full range of your possessions—from old dishcloth to Oriental rug—are fair game in the eyes of a teething pup. Puppies are not all that discerning when it comes to finding something to literally 'sink their teeth into'—everything tastes great!

Jack Russell puppies are fairly aggressive chewers and only the hardest, strongest toys should be offered to them. Breeders advise owners to resist stuffed toys, because they can become de-stuffed in no time. The overly excited pup may ingest the stuffing, which is neither digestible nor nutritious.

Similarly, squeaky toys are quite popular, but must be avoided for the Jack Russell. Perhaps a squeaky toy can be used as an aid in training, but not for free play. If a pup 'disembowels' one of these, the small plastic squeaker inside can be dangerous if swallowed. Monitor the condition of all your pup's toys carefully and get rid of any that have been

**Do not give your Jack Russell Terrier soft vinyl toys made for children. Rely upon your local pet shop to supply you with a suitable chew device for your dog.**

Jack Russells are aggressive chewers and can be very possessive of their toys.

chewed to the point of becoming potentially dangerous.

Be careful of natural bones, which have a tendency to splinter into sharp, dangerous pieces. Also be careful of rawhide, which can turn into pieces that are easy to swallow or into a mushy mess on your carpet.

### Lead

A nylon lead is probably the best option as it is the most resistant to puppy teeth should your pup take a liking to chewing on his lead. Of course, this is a habit that should be nipped in the bud, but if your pup likes to chew on his lead he has a very slim chance of being able to chew through the strong nylon. Nylon leads are also lightweight, which is good for a young Jack Russell who is just getting used to the idea of walking on a lead. For everyday walking and safety purposes, the nylon lead is a good choice. As your pup grows up and gets used to walking on the lead, you may want to purchase a flexible lead. These leads allow you to extend the length to give the dog a broader area to explore or to shorten the length to keep the close to you. Of

Did You Know?

The cost of food must also be mentioned. All dogs need a good quality food with an adequate supply of protein to develop their bones and muscles properly. Most dogs are not picky eaters but unless fed properly they can quickly succumb to skin problems.

course there are special leads for training purposes, but these are not necessary for routine walks.

### Collar

Your pup should get used to wearing a collar all the time since you will want to attach his ID tags to it. Plus, the lead and collar go hand in hand—you have to attach the lead to something! A lightweight nylon collar is a good choice; make sure that it fits snugly enough so that the pup cannot wriggle out of it, but is loose enough so that it will not be uncomfortably tight around the pup's neck. You should be able to fit a finger between the pup and the collar. It may take some time for your pup to get used to wearing the collar, but soon he will not even notice that it is there. Choke collars are made for training, but should only be used by an experienced handler.

### Food and Water Bowls

Your pup will need two bowls, one for food and one for water. You may want two sets of bowls, one for inside and one for outside, depending on where the dog will be fed and where he will be spending most of his time. Stainless steel or sturdy plastic bowls are popular choices. Plastic bowls are more chewable. Dogs tend not to chew on the steel variety, which can be sterilised. It is important to buy sturdy bowls since anything is in danger of being chewed by puppy teeth and you do not want your dog to be constantly chewing apart his bowl (for his safety and for your purse!).

### Cleaning Supplies

Until a pup is housetrained you will be doing a lot of cleaning. Accidents will occur, which is okay in the beginning because the puppy does not know any

**Both heavy plastic and stainless steel bowls are available for your Jack Russell.**

# Choose the Proper Collar for Your Dog

The BUCKLE COLLAR is the standard collar used for everyday purpose. Be sure that you adjust the buckle on growing puppies. Check it every day. It can become too tight overnight! These collars can be made of leather or nylon. Attach your dog's identification tags to this collar.

Buckle Collar

The CHOKE COLLAR is the usual collar recommended for training. It is constructed of highly polished steel so that it slides easily through the stainless steel loop. The idea is that the dog controls the pressure around its neck and he will stop pulling if the collar becomes uncomfortable. Never leave a choke collar on your dog when not training.

Choke Collar

The HALTER is for a trained dog that has to be restrained to prevent running away, chasing a cat and the like. Considered the most humane of all collars, it is frequently used on smaller dogs for which collars are not comfortable.

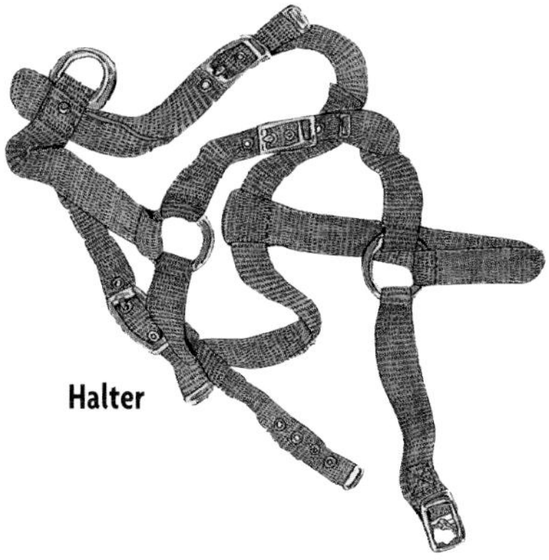

Halter

**Your local pet shop will have a wide variety of plastic food and water bowls for your Jack Russell Terrier. If your dog is a destructive chewer, you will need something more sturdy such as stainless steel.**

Photo courtesy of Mikki Pet Products.

better. All you can do is be prepared to clean up any 'accidents.' Old rags, towels, newspapers and a safe disinfectant are good to have on hand.

### Beyond the Basics

The items previously discussed are the bare necessities. You will find out what else you need as you go along—grooming supplies, flea/tick protection, baby gates to partition a room, etc. These things will vary depending on your situation but it is important that you have everything you need to feed and make your Jack Russell comfortable in his first few days at home.

## PUPPY-PROOFING YOUR HOME

Aside from making sure that your Jack Russell will be comfortable in your home, you also have to make sure that your home is safe for your Jack Russell. This means taking precautions that your pup will not get into anything he should not get into and that there is nothing within his reach that may harm him should he sniff it, chew it, inspect it, etc. This probably seems obvious since, whilst you are primarily concerned with your pup's safety, at the same time you do not want your belongings to be ruined. Breakables should be placed out of reach if your dog is to have full run of the house. If he is to be limited to certain places within the house, keep any potentially dangerous items in the 'off-limits' areas. An electrical cord can pose a danger should the puppy decide to taste it—and who is going to convince a pup that it would not make a great chew toy?

## Financial Responsibility

Grooming tools, collars, leashes, dog beds and, of course, toys will be an expense to you when you first obtain your pup, and the cost will continue throughout your dog's lifetime. If your puppy damages or destroys your possessions (as most puppies surely will!) or something belonging to a neighbour, you can calculate additional expense. There is also flea and pest control, which every dog owner faces more than once. You must be able to handle the financial responsibility of owning a dog.

## Natural Toxins

Examine your grass and garden landscaping before bringing your puppy home. Many varieties of plants have leaves, stems or flowers that are toxic if ingested, and you can depend on a curious puppy to investigate them. Ask your veterinarian for information on poisonous plants or research them at your library.

Cords should be fastened tightly against the wall. If your dog is going to spend time in a crate, make sure that there is nothing near his crate that he can reach if he sticks his curious little nose or paws through the openings. Just as you would with a child, keep all household cleaners and chemicals where the pup cannot get to them.

It is also important to make sure that the outside of your home is safe. Of course your puppy should never be unsupervised, but a pup let loose in the garden will want to run and explore, and he should be granted that freedom. Do not let a fence give you a false sense of security; you would be surprised how crafty (and persistent) a dog can be in working out how to dig under and squeeze his way through small holes, or to jump or climb over a fence. The remedy is to make the fence high enough so that it really is impossible for your dog to get over it (about 3 metres should suffice), and well embedded into the ground. Be sure to repair or secure any gaps in the fence. Check the fence periodically to ensure that it is in good shape and make repairs as needed; a very determined pup may return to the same spot to 'work on it' until he is able to get through. Jack Russells are very talented diggers; keep this in mind.

## Did You Know?

Some experts in canine health advise that stress during a dog's early years of development can compromise and weaken his immune system and may trigger the potential for a shortened life expectancy. They emphasise the need for happy and stress-free growing-up years.

## Chemical Toxins

Scour your garage for potential puppy dangers. Remove weed killers, pesticides and antifreeze materials. Antifreeze is highly toxic and even a few drops can kill an adult dog. The sweet taste attracts the animal, who will quickly consume it from the floor or curbside.

**FIRST TRIP TO THE VET**

You have picked out your puppy, and your home and family are ready. Now all you have to do is collect your Jack Russell from the breeder and the fun begins, right? Well...not so fast. Something else you need to prepare is your pup's first trip to the veterinary surgeon. Perhaps the breeder can recommend someone in the area that specialises in Jack Russells, or maybe you know some other Jack Russell owners who can suggest a good vet. Either way, you should have an appointment arranged for your pup before you pick him up and plan on taking him for an examination before bringing him home.

The pup's first visit will consist of an overall examination to make sure that the pup does not have any problems that are not apparent to the eye.

## Puppy-Proofing

Thoroughly puppy-proof your house before bringing your puppy home. Never use roach or rodent poisons in any area accessible to the puppy. Avoid the use of toilet bowl cleaners. Most dogs are born with toilet bowl sonar and will take a drink if the lid is left open. Also keep the rubbish secured and out of reach.

## Did You Know?

Taking your dog from the breeder to your home in a car can be a very uncomfortable experience for both of you. The puppy will have been taken from his warm, friendly, safe environment and brought into a strange new environment. An environment that moves! Be prepared for loose bowels, urination, crying, whining and even fear biting. With proper love and encouragement when you arrive home, the stress of the trip should quickly disappear.

**Select a veterinary surgeon convenient to your home in case you have to reach her in an emergency. A local vet is always more convenient than a distant one, especially when you have an ailing puppy or pregnant bitch.**

The veterinary surgeon will also set up a schedule for the pup's vaccinations; the breeder will inform you of which ones the pup has already received and the vet can continue from there.

Children and dogs are natural friends. It is good training for the children to have a big part in the selection, care and training of the family dog.

**INTRODUCTION TO THE FAMILY**

Everyone in the house will be excited about the puppy coming home and will want to pet him and play with him, but it is best to make the introduction low-key so as not to overwhelm the puppy. He is apprehensive already. It is the first time he has been separated from his mother and the breeder, and the ride to your home is likely the first time he has been in a car. The last thing you want to do is smother him, as this will only frighten him further. This is not to say that human contact is not extremely necessary at this stage, because this is the time when a connection between the pup and his human family is formed. Gentle petting and soothing words should help console him, as well as just putting him down and letting him explore on his own (under your watchful eye, of course).

The pup may approach the family members or may busy himself with exploring for a while. Gradually, each person should spend some time with the pup, one at a time, crouching down to get as close

### Did You Know?

It will take at least two weeks for your puppy to become accustomed to his new surroundings. Give him

lots of love, attention, handling, frequent opportunities to relieve himself, a diet he likes to eat and a place he can call his own.

to the pup's level as possible and letting him sniff their hands and petting him gently. He definitely needs human attention and he needs to be touched—this is how to form an immediate bond. Just remember that the pup is experiencing a lot of things for the first time, at the same time. There are new people, new noises, new smells, and new things to investigate: so be gentle, be affectionate, and be as comforting as you can be.

## Information . . .

**You will probably start feeding your pup the same food that he has been getting from the breeder; the breeder should give you a few days' supply to start you off.**

**Although you should not give your pup too many treats, you will want to have puppy treats on hand for coaxing, training, rewards, etc. Be careful, though, as a small pup's calorie requirements are relatively low and a few treats can add up to almost a full day's worth of calories without the required nutrition.**

### YOUR PUP'S FIRST NIGHT HOME

You have travelled home with your new charge safely in his basket or crate. He's been to the vet for a thorough check-up; he's been weighed, his papers examined; perhaps he's even been vaccinated and wormed as well. He's met the family, licked the whole family, including the excited children and the less-than-happy cat. He's explored his

**Give your new Jack Russell Terrier a soft toy, something cuddly, for his first night in his new home. You won't want something so easily torn once the dog starts chewing intently.**

## Did You Know?

An important consideration to be discussed is the sex of your puppy. For a family companion, a bitch

may be the better choice, considering the female's inbred concern for all young creatures and her accompanying tolerance and patience. It is always advisable to spay a pet bitch, which may guarantee her a longer life.

area, his new bed, the garden and anywhere else he's been permitted. He's eaten his first meal at home and relieved himself in the proper place. He's heard lots of new sounds, smelled new friends and seen more of the outside world than ever before.

That was just the first day! He's worn out and is ready for bed…or so you think!

It's puppy's first night and you are ready to say 'Good night'—keep in mind that this is puppy's first night ever to be sleeping alone. His dam and littermates are no longer at paw's length and he's a bit scared, cold and lonely. Be reassuring to your new family member. This is not the time to spoil him and give in to his inevitable whining.

Puppies whine. They whine to let the others know where they are and hopefully to get company out of it. Place your pup in his new bed or crate in his room and close the door. Mercifully, he may fall asleep without a peep. If the inevitable occurs, ignore the whining: he is fine. Be strong and keep his interest in mind. Do not allow your heart to become guilty and visit the pup. He will fall asleep.

Many breeders recommend placing a piece of bedding from his former homestead in his new bed so that he recognises the scent of his littermates. Others

Introduce your Jack Russell Terrier puppies to other dogs but be sure the other dogs are socialised themselves. A non-dog-aggressive breed like the Golden Retriever is a good choice.

still advise placing a hot water bottle in his bed for warmth. This latter may be a good idea provided the pup doesn't attempt to suckle—he'll get good and wet and may not fall asleep so fast.

Puppy's first night can be somewhat stressful for the pup and his new family. Remember that you are setting the tone of night-time at your house. Unless you want to play with your pup every evening at 10 p.m., midnight and 2 a.m., don't initiate the habit. Your family will thank you, and so will your pup!

## PREVENTING PUPPY PROBLEMS

### SOCIALISATION

Now that you have done all of the preparatory work and have helped your pup get accustomed to his new home and family, it is about time for you to have some fun! Socialising your Jack Russell pup gives you the opportunity to show off your new friend, and your pup gets to reap the benefits of being an adorable furry creature that people will want to pet and, in general, think is absolutely precious!

Besides getting to know his new family, your puppy should be exposed to other people, animals and situations, but of course he must not come into close contact with dogs you don't know well until his course of injections is fully complete. This will help him become well adjusted as he grows up and less prone to

## Socialisation

**Thorough socialisation includes not only meeting new people but also being introduced to new experiences such as riding in the car, having his coat**

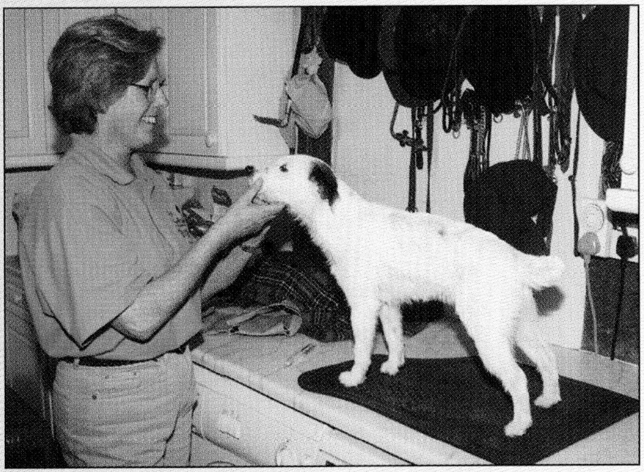

**brushed, hearing the television, walking in a crowd—the list is endless. The more your pup experiences, and the more positive the experiences are, the less of a shock and the less scary it will be for your pup to encounter new things.**

## Training Tip

**Training your puppy takes much patience and can be frustrating at times, but you should see results from**

**your efforts. If you have a puppy that seems untrainable, take him to a trainer or behaviourist. The dog may have a personality problem that requires the help of a professional, or perhaps you need help in learning how to train your dog.**

being timid or fearful of the new things he will encounter. Your pup's socialisation began with the breeder but now it is your responsibility to continue it. The socialisation he receives up until the age of 12 weeks is the most critical, as this is the time when he forms his impressions of the outside world. Be especially careful during the eight-to-ten-week period, also known as the fear period. The interaction he receives during this time should be gentle and reassuring. Lack of socialisation can manifest itself in fear and aggression as the dog grows up. He needs lots of human contact, affection, handling and exposure to other animals.

Once your pup has received his necessary vaccinations, feel free to take him out and about (on his lead, of course). Walk him around the neighbourhood, take him on your daily errands, let people pet him, let him meet other dogs and pets, etc. Puppies do not have to try to make friends; there will be no shortage of people who will want to introduce themselves. Just make sure that you carefully supervise each meeting. If the neighbourhood children want to say hello, for example, that is great—children and pups most often make great companions. However, sometimes an excited child can unintentionally handle a pup too roughly, or an overzealous pup can playfully nip a little too hard. You want to make socialisation experiences positive ones. What a pup learns during this very formative stage will impact his attitude toward future encounters. You want your dog to be comfortable around everyone. A pup that has a bad experience with a child may grow up to be a dog that is shy around or aggressive toward children.

### Consistency in Training

Dogs, being pack animals, naturally need a leader or else they try to establish dominance in their packs. When you bring a dog into your family, the choice of who becomes the leader and who becomes the 'pack' is entirely up to you! Your pup's intuitive quest for dominance, coupled with the fact that it is nearly impossible to look at an adorable Jack Russell pup with his 'puppy-dog' eyes and not cave in, give the pup almost an unfair advantage in getting the upper hand! A pup will definitely test the waters to see what he can and cannot do. Do not give in to those pleading eyes—stand your ground when it comes to disciplining the pup and make sure that all family members do the same. It will only confuse the pup when Mother tells him to get off the sofa when he is used to sitting up there with Father to watch the nightly news. Avoid discrepancies by having all members of the household decide on the rules before the pup even comes home...and be consistent in enforcing them! Early training shapes the dog's personality, so you cannot be unclear in what you expect.

## COMMON PUPPY PROBLEMS

The best way to prevent puppy problems is to be proactive in stopping an undesirable behaviour as soon as it starts. The old saying 'You can't teach an old dog new tricks' does not necessarily hold true, but it is true that it is much easier to discourage bad behaviour in a young developing pup than to wait until the pup's bad behaviour becomes the adult dog's bad habit. There are some problems that are especially prevalent in puppies as they develop.

### NIPPING

As puppies start to teethe, they feel the need to sink their teeth into anything available... unfortunately that includes

### Did You Know?

The majority of problems that is commonly seen in young pups will disappear as your dog gets older. However, how you deal with problems when he is young will determine how he reacts to discipline as an adult dog. It is important to establish who is boss (hopefully it will be you!) right away when you are first bonding with your dog. This bond will set the tone for the rest of your life together.

## Chewing Tips

Chewing goes hand in hand with nipping in the sense that a teething puppy is always looking for a way to soothe his aching gums. In this case, instead of chewing on you, he may have taken a liking to your favourite shoe or something else which he should not be chewing. Again, realise that this is a normal canine behaviour that does not need to be discouraged, only redirected. Your pup just needs to be taught what is acceptable to chew on and what is off limits. Consistently

tell him NO when you catch him chewing on something forbidden and give him a chew toy. Conversely, praise him when you catch him chewing on something appropriate. In this way you are discouraging the inappropriate behaviour and reinforcing the desired behaviour. The puppy chewing should stop after his adult teeth have come in, but an adult dog continues to chew for various reasons—perhaps because he is bored, perhaps to relieve tension or perhaps he just likes to chew. That is why it is important to redirect his chewing when he is still young.

your fingers, arms, hair, and toes. You may find this behaviour cute for the first five seconds...until you feel just how sharp those puppy teeth are. This is something you want to discourage immediately and consistently with a firm 'No!' (or whatever number of firm 'No's' it takes for him to understand that you mean business). Then replace your finger with an appropriate chew toy. Whilst this behaviour is merely annoying when the dog is young, it can become dangerous as your Jack Russell's adult teeth grow in and his jaws develop, and he continues to think it is okay to gnaw on human appendages. Your Jack Russell does not mean any harm with a friendly nip, but he also does not know his own strength.

### Crying/Whining

Your pup will often cry, whine, whimper, howl or make some type of commotion when he is left alone. This is basically his way of calling out for attention to make sure that you know he is there and that you have not forgotten about him. He feels insecure when he is left alone, when you are out of the house and he is in his crate or when you are in another part of the house and he cannot see you. The noise he is making is an expression of the anxiety he feels at being alone, so he needs to be taught that being alone is okay. You are not actually training the dog to stop making noise, you are training him to feel comfortable when he is alone and thus removing the need for him to make the noise. This is where the crate filled with cosy bedding and a toy comes in handy. You want to know that he is safe when you are not there to supervise, and you know that he will be safe in his crate rather than roaming freely about the house. In order for the pup to stay in his crate without making a fuss, he needs to be comfortable in his crate. On that note, it is extremely important that the crate is never used as a form of punishment, or the pup will have a negative association with the crate.

Accustom the pup to the crate in short, gradually increasing time intervals in which you put him in the crate, maybe with a treat, and stay in the room with him. If he cries or makes a fuss, do not go to him, but stay in his sight. Gradually he will realise that staying in his crate is all right without your help, and it will not be so traumatic for him when you are not around. You may want to leave the radio on softly when you leave the house; the sound of human voices may be comforting to him.

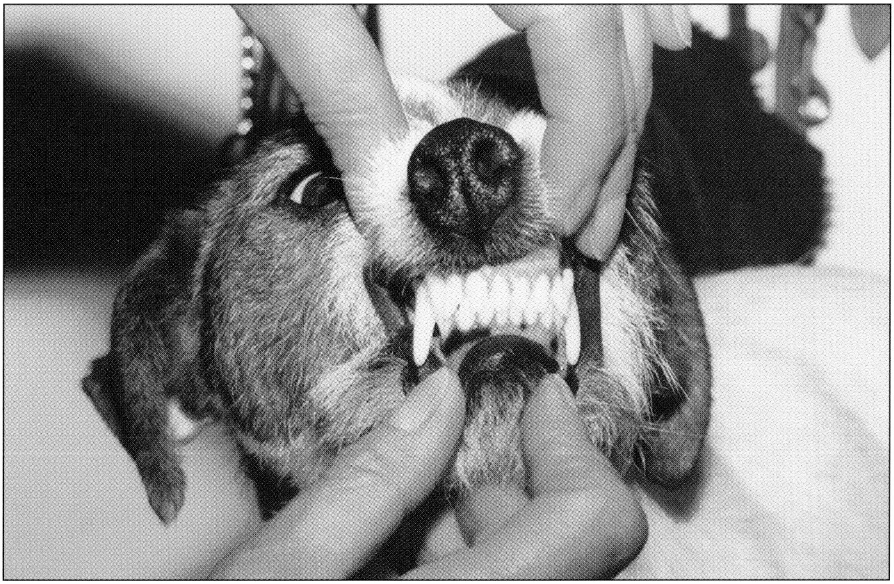

**It is easy to see why Jack Russell Terriers are such aggressive chewers. They have large teeth for such a small breed. Sometimes a dog will nip playfully, without aggression, perhaps to get your attention. But with canine teeth like those shown here, that could be a dangerous encounter.**

EVERYDAY CARE OF YOUR

# PARSON JACK RUSSELL TERRIER

Puppies will eat whatever food you offer. They cannot make a decision about quality. You have to decide on the healthiest diet available for your puppy. Seek advice from your vet or the breeder from whom you bought the puppy.

## DIETARY AND FEEDING CONSIDERATIONS

Today the choices of food for your Jack Russell are many and varied. There are simply dozens of brands of food in all sorts of flavours and textures, ranging from puppy diets to those for seniors. There are even hypoallergenic and low-calorie diets available. Because your Jack Russell's food has a bearing on coat, health and temperament, it is essential that the most suitable diet be selected for a Jack Russell of his age. It is fair to say, however, that even dedicated owners can be somewhat perplexed by the enormous range of foods available. Only understanding what is best for your dog will help you reach a valued decision.

Dog foods are produced in three basic types: dried, semi-moist and tinned. Dried foods are useful for the cost-conscious for overall they tend to be less expensive than semi-moist or tinned. These contain the least fat and the most preservatives. In general, tinned foods are made up of 60–70 percent water, whilst semi-moist ones often contain so much sugar that they are perhaps the least preferred by owners, even though their dogs seem to like them.

When selecting your dog's diet, three stages of development must be considered: the puppy stage, adult stage and the senior or veteran stage.

### Did You Know?

A good test for proper diet is the colour, odour and firmness of your dog's stool. A healthy dog usually produces three semi-hard stools per day. The stools should have no unpleasant odour. They should be the same colour from excretion to excretion.

**PUPPY STAGE**

Puppies instinctively want to suck milk from their mother's teats and a normal puppy will exhibit this behaviour from just a few moments following birth. If puppies do not attempt to suckle within the first half-hour or so, they should be encouraged to do so by placing them on the nipples, having selected ones with plenty of milk. This early milk supply is important in providing colostrum to protect the puppies during the first eight to ten weeks of their lives. Although a mother's milk is much better than any milk formula, despite there being some excellent ones available, if the puppies do not feed you will have to feed them yourself. For those with less experience, advice from

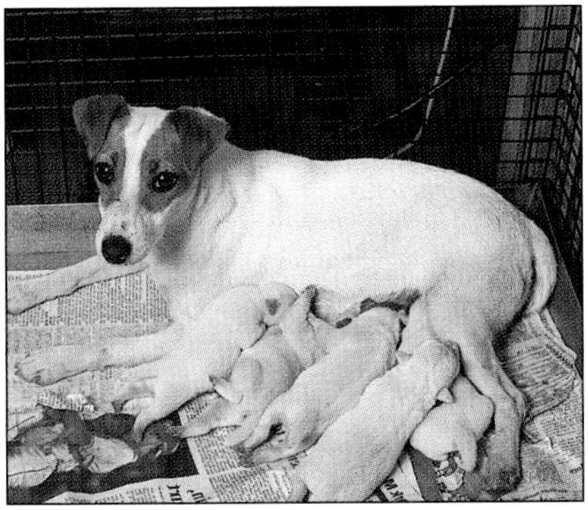

Jack Russell Terrier puppies should be allowed to nurse from their mothers for the first six weeks of their lives.

a veterinary surgeon is important so that you feed not only the right quantity of milk but that of correct quality, fed at suitably frequent intervals, usually every two hours

## Food Preference

Selecting the best dried dog food is difficult. There is no majority consensus amongst veterinary scientists as to the value of

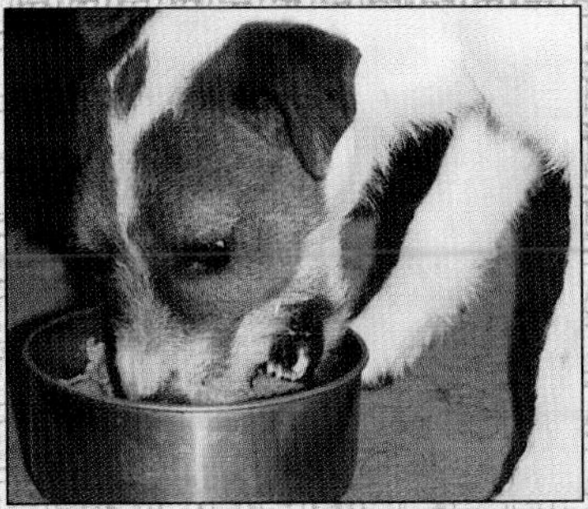

nutrient analyses (protein, fat, fibre, moisture, ash, cholesterol, minerals, etc.). All agree that feeding trials are what matters, but you also have to consider the individual dog. Its weight, age, activity and what pleases its taste, all must be considered. It is probably best to take the advice of your veterinary surgeon. Every dog's dietary requirements vary, even during the lifetime of a particular dog.

If your dog is fed a good dried food, it does not require supplements of meat or vegetables. Dogs do appreciate a little variety in their diets so you may choose to stay with the same brand, but vary the flavour. Alternatively you may wish to add a little flavoured stock to give a difference to the taste.

**There is no true substitute for mother's milk during the first few weeks of a pup's life. By the time the puppies are two months old they should be fully weaned from their dam.**

## Did You Know?

Dog food must be at room temperature, neither too hot nor too cold. Fresh water, changed daily and served in a clean bowl, is mandatory, especially when feeding dried food.

Never feed your dog from the table while you are eating. Never feed your dog left-overs from your own meal. They usually contain too much fat and too much seasoning.

Dogs must chew their food. Hard pellets are excellent; soups and slurries are to be avoided.

Don't add left-overs or any extras to normal dog food. The

normal food is usually balanced and adding something extra destroys the balance.

Except for age-related changes, dogs do not require dietary variations. They can be fed the same diet, day after day, without their becoming ill.

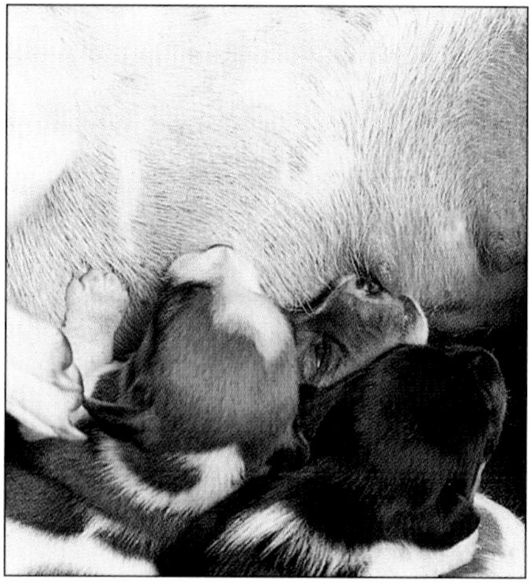

during the first few days of life.

Puppies should be allowed to nurse from their mothers for about the first six weeks, although from the third or fourth week you will have begun to introduce small portions of suitable solid food. Most breeders like to introduce alternate milk and meat meals initially, building up to weaning time.

By the time the puppies are seven or a maximum of eight weeks old, they should be fully weaned and fed solely on a proprietary puppy food. Selection of the most suitable, good-quality diet at this time is essential, for a puppy's fastest growth rate is during the first year of life. Veterinary surgeons are usually able to offer advice in this regard and, although the frequency of meals will have been reduced over time, only

## Did You Know?

You must store your dried dog food carefully. Open packages of dog food quickly lose their vitamin value, usually within 90 days of being opened. Mould spores and vermin could also contaminate the food.

when a young dog has reached the age of about 18 months should an adult diet be fed.

Puppy and junior diets should be well balanced for the needs of your dog, so that except in certain circumstances additional vitamins, minerals and proteins will not be required.

### Adult Diets

A dog is considered an adult when it has stopped growing, so in general the diet of a Jack Russell can be changed to an adult one at about 12 months of age. However, your Jack Russell will not achieve physical and mental maturity until 18 months or later. Again you should rely upon your veterinary surgeon or dietary specialist to recommend an acceptable maintenance diet. Major dog food manufacturers specialise in this type of food, and it is just necessary for you to select the one best suited to your dog's needs. Jack Russells, which are generally very active dogs, may have different requirements than sedate dogs.

### Senior Diets

As dogs get older, their metabolism changes. The older dog usually exercises less, moves more slowly and sleeps more. This change in lifestyle and physiological performance requires a change in diet. Since these changes take place slowly,

## Grain-Based Diets

**Many adult diets are based on grain. There is nothing wrong with this as long as it does not contain soy meal. Diets based on soy often cause flatulence (passing gas).**

**Grain-based diets are almost always the least expensive and a good grain diet is just as good as the most expensive diet containing animal protein.**

**There are many cases, however, when your dog might require a special diet. These special requirements should only be recommended by your veterinary surgeon.**

# What are you feeding your dog?

**Read the label on your dog food. Many dog foods only advise what 50–55% of the contents are, leaving the other 45% in doubt.**

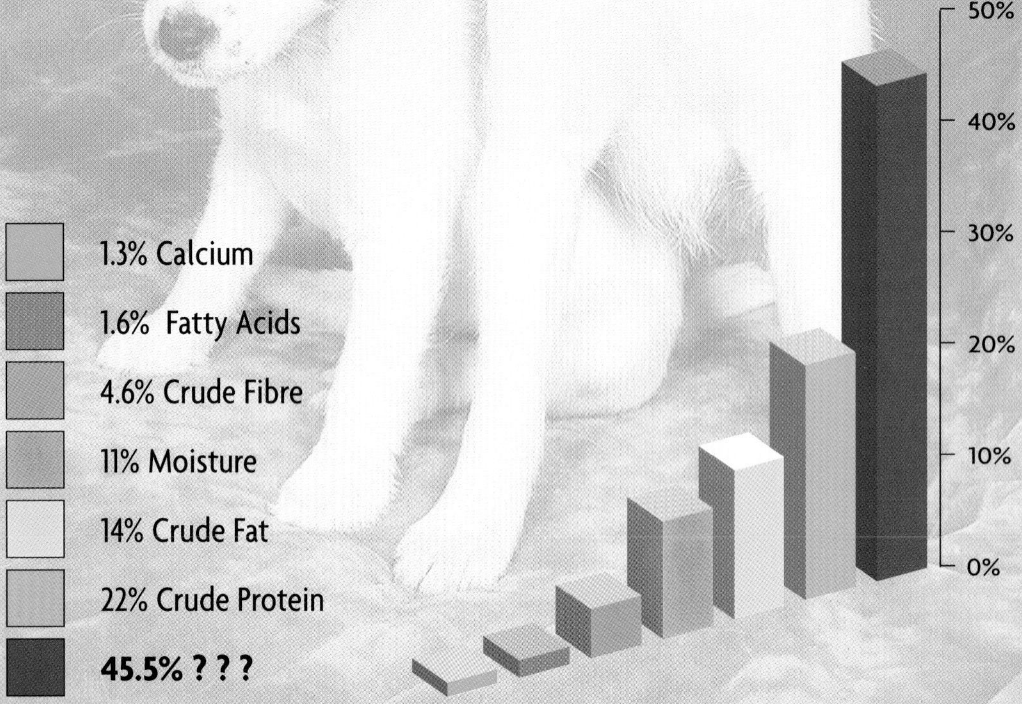

they might not be recognisable. What is easily recognisable is weight gain. By continuing to feed your dog an adult-maintenance diet when it is slowing down metabolically, your dog will gain weight. Obesity in an older dog compounds the health problems that already accompany old age.

As your dog gets older, few of his organs function up to par. The kidneys slow down and the intestines become less efficient. These age-related factors are best handled with a change in diet and a change in feeding schedule to give smaller portions that are more easily digested.

There is no single best diet for every older dog. Whilst many dogs do well on light or senior diets, other dogs do better on puppy diets or other special premium diets such as lamb and rice. Be sensitive to your senior Jack Russell's diet and this will help control other problems that may arise with your old friend.

**WATER**

Just as your dog needs proper nutrition from his food, water is an essential 'nutrient' as well. Water keeps the dog's body properly hydrated and promotes normal function of the body's systems. During housebreaking it is necessary to keep an eye on how much water your Jack Russell is drinking, but once he is reliably trained he should have access to clean fresh water at all times. Make sure that the dog's water bowl is clean, and change the water often, making sure that water is always available for your dog, especially if you feed dried food.

## Information . . .

**You should be careful where you exercise your dog. Many countryside areas have been sprayed with chemicals that are highly toxic to both dogs and humans. Never allow your dog to eat grass or drink from puddles on either public or private grounds, as the run-off water may contain chemicals from sprays and herbicides.**

**EXERCISE**

Although a Jack Russell is small, he is active and will not be happy without plenty of exercise. A sedentary lifestyle is as harmful to a dog as it is to a person even more so in a naturally active breed. The Jack Russell is energetic and athletic, but you don't have be be an Olympic athlete to own one. Regular walks, play sessions in the garden or letting the dog run free in the garden under your supervision are sufficient forms of exercise for the

The Jack Russell Terrier appears in rough and smooth coat. Both varieties cast coat and require a bit of daily brushing. The rough coat requires extensive work in order for it to appear well groomed.

Jack Russell. For those who are more ambitious, you will find that your Jack Russell also enjoys long walks, an occasional hike, games of fetch or even a swim! Bear in mind that an overweight dog should never be suddenly over-exercised; instead he should be allowed to increase slowly how much he exercises.

Not only is exercise essential to keep the dog's body fit, it is essential to his mental well-being. A bored dog will find something to do, which often manifests itself in some type of destructive behaviour. With the Jack Russell, this can often mean digging. In this sense, it is essential for the owner's mental well being as well!

**GROOMING**

Do understand when purchasing a dog that you have the responsibility of maintaining your dog. Think of it in terms of your child—you bathe your youngster, comb his hair and put a clean set of clothes on him. The end product is that you have a child that smells good, looks nice and that you enjoy having in your company. It is the same with your dog—keep the dog brushed, cleaned and trimmed, and you will find it a pleasure to be in his company.

The Jack Russell Terrier comes in two coat types: the rough coat and the smooth coat. Both coat types shed and will require some maintenance, but the smooth coat is easier to keep up than the rough coat.

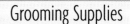

## Grooming Supplies

How much grooming equipment you purchase will depend on how much grooming you are going to do. Here are some basics:

- Natural bristle brush
- Slicker brush
- Metal comb
- Hound glove (smooth coat)
- Stripping knife (rough coat)
- Grooming table
- Scissors
- Blaster
- Rubber mat
- Dog shampoo
- Spray hose attachment
- Ear cleaner
- Cotton wipes
- Towels
- Nail clippers

### Grooming the Smooth Coat

For those with a smooth-coated Jack Russell Terrier, grooming will consist of primarily a weekly 'go-over' brushing. Brush him down with a bristle brush or glove. Take a damp wash cloth and wipe down the entire body. Once a month or so you may want to give him a bath. You will find that this will loosen any dead coat, so after the bath be sure to brush him out thoroughly in order to clean out any dead undercoat. After the dog is bathed, this is also a good time to trim the toenails as they will be soft and easier to trim. You may want to trim the whiskers to the skin as this will give the dog a neat, clean-cut look. Wipe him dry with a towel or use a blaster, or if it is a nice, sunny day, you may want to put him on the patio to dry.

If you are showing your smooth-coated Jack Russell, you may want to rub the dog down

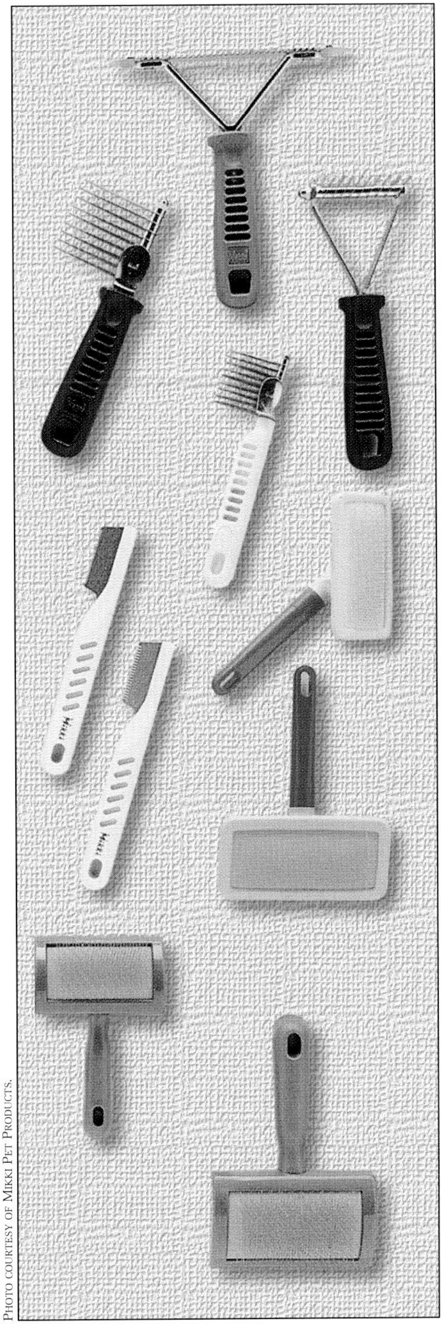

Photo courtesy of Mikki Pet Products.

**Your local pet shop should specialise in dog grooming tools. Discuss your Jack Russell's needs for brushes, nail clippers and stripping knives, plus whatever else is recommended.**

**Early acclimatisation to the grooming table results in a Jack Russell who will stand politely for grooming and examination by a show judge.**

Normal terrier hairs showing uniform, clean cuticles (outer covering). These photos are magnified 560 times. The inset shows a crushed hair magnified 140 times.

S.E.M. By Dr Dennis Kunkel, University of Hawaii

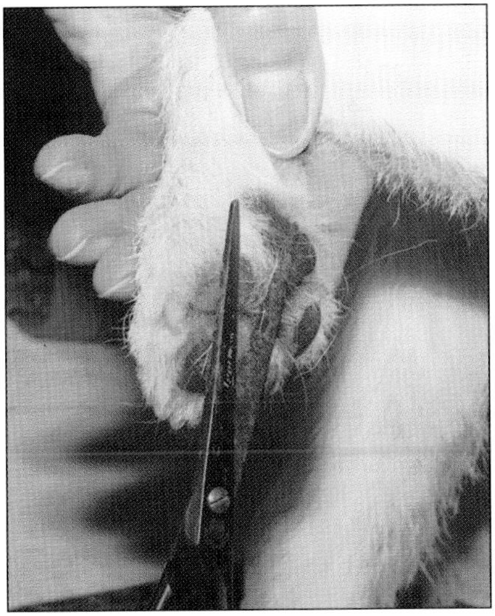

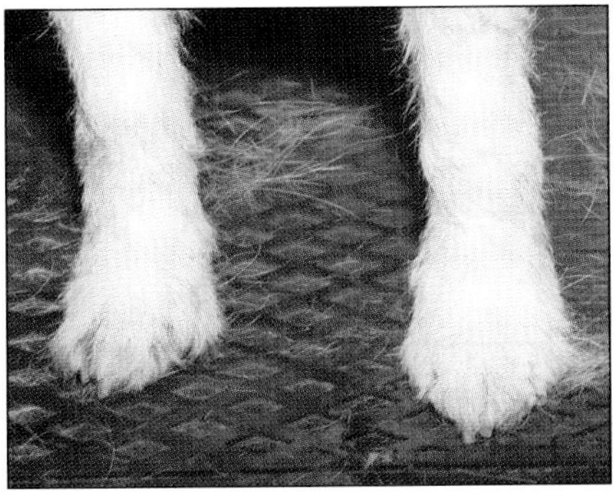

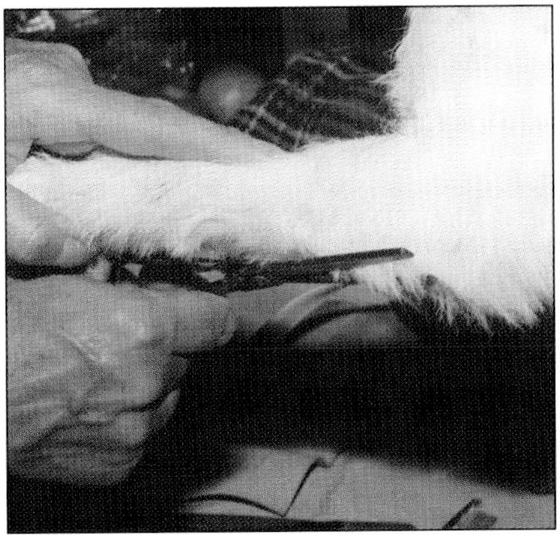

with a pomade or some other hair dressing to give his coat a high gloss. Trimming for show on a smooth coat will be minimal and the purpose will be to neaten up the dog. Smooth-coated dogs are low maintenance, and those of us who own one appreciate it!

**The thick hair on the bottom of the Jack Russell's feet must be trimmed.**

### Grooming the Rough Coat

The rough-coated dog will require more grooming, and if you are planning to show your rough-coated Jack Russell Terrier, you will be ahead of the game if you purchase your puppy from a reputable breeder who grooms and shows her dogs. If so, this is the individual to see for grooming lessons to learn how to get your dog ready for the show ring. Grooming for the show is an art, and an art that cannot be learned in only a few months.

**The feet should be neat with the toenails showing.**

The rough-coated Jack Russell needs to be neatened up in appearance before entering the show ring. If the coat is not paid the proper attention, it will become very shaggy in appearance and the dog will not present the correct smartness in the ring that is required. The coat should be plucked, taking out the longer and dead hairs and allowing a new harsh coat to grow back in its place. The coat on the legs, muzzle and chest should be left longer but neatened up.

**Your Jack Russell's coat doesn't need much shaping but scissors can be used to trim the feathering hair on the legs.**

The desired coat can only be acquired by stripping the body

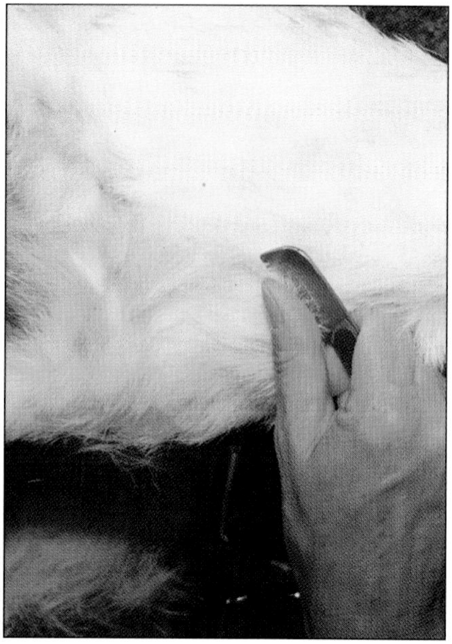

Using a stripping knife requires skill and experience. Consider using a professional groomer several times a year.

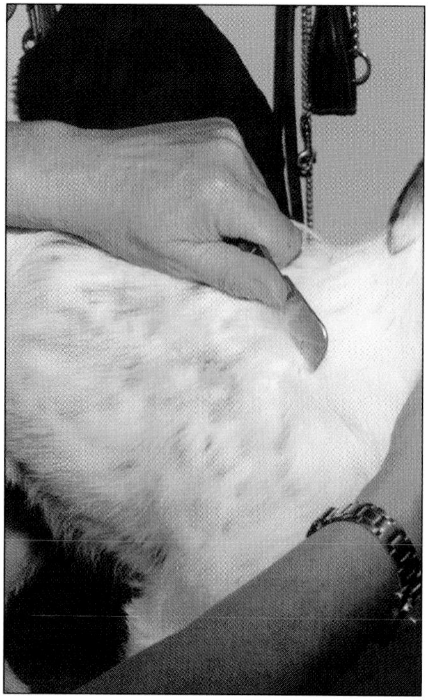

Stripping the top of the dog is usually where beginners learn.

coat with a stripping knife or stripping by hand. Within 8 to 10 weeks, and with the proper upkeep, he will have grown from his 'underwear' outfit stage into a smart new outfit ready for the ring. This all takes skill, time and interest in order to do it well.

Pet grooming is different from grooming for the show ring, as you can use scissors or a clipper for trimming the body and the furnishings. You will have a neat, clean and trimmed dog that will still look like a Jack Russell Terrier, but he will not have the harsh coat required for the show ring. Even those with kennels who are active in the show ring will clip their old dogs or those who are no longer being shown.

An important piece of equipment if you plan to groom your rough-coated Jack Russell at home is a grooming table, something sturdy with a rubber mat covering the top. You will need a grooming arm, or a 'hanger.' (You can use a table in your laundry room with an eyehook in the ceiling for holding the leash.) Your dog will now be comfortable even if confined and you will be able to work on the dog. Grooming is a very difficult and frustrating job if you try to groom without a table and a grooming arm. You will also need a metal comb, a slicker brush, a good, sharp pair of scissors and a toenail trimmer.

To start, set your dog on the table and put the leash around his neck. Have your leash up behind the ears and have the leash taut when you fasten it to your eyehook. Do not walk away and leave your dog unattended as he can jump off the table and be left dangling from the leash with his feet scrambling around in the air.

Take your slicker brush and brush out the entire coat. Brush the whiskers toward the nose, the body hair toward the tail, and the tail up toward the tip of the tail. Brush the leg furnishings up toward the body and brush the chest hair down toward the table. Hold the dog up by the front legs and gently brush the stomach hair, first toward the head and then back toward the rear. For cleanliness, you may want to take your scissors and trim the area around the penis. With the girls, trim some of the hair around the vulva.

Now that your dog is brushed out, comb through the coat with your metal comb. By now you have removed a fair amount of dead hair and your dog will already be looking better. You may find some small mats and these can be worked out with your fingers or your comb. If you brush your dog out every week or so, you will not have too much of a problem with the mats.

Take your scissors or stripping knife and trim off anything that 'sticks out.' If this is your first experience, you may be a bit clumsy, but the hair will grow back in a short time. The finished product may not be quite what you had expected, but expertise will come with experience and you will soon be very proud of your efforts. Your dog should now look like what a rough-coated Jack Russell Terrier should look like.

**You can bath your Jack Russell inside or out doors. Never bath your dog outside in inclement weather.**

Put your dog in the laundry tub when you are finished and give him a good bath and rinsing. A shower or hose attachment is necessary for thoroughly wetting and rinsing the coat. Check the water temperature to make sure that it is neither too hot nor too cold.

Next, apply shampoo to the dog's coat and work it into a good lather. You should purchase a shampoo that is made for dogs. Do not use a product made for human hair. Wash the head last; you do not want shampoo to drip into the

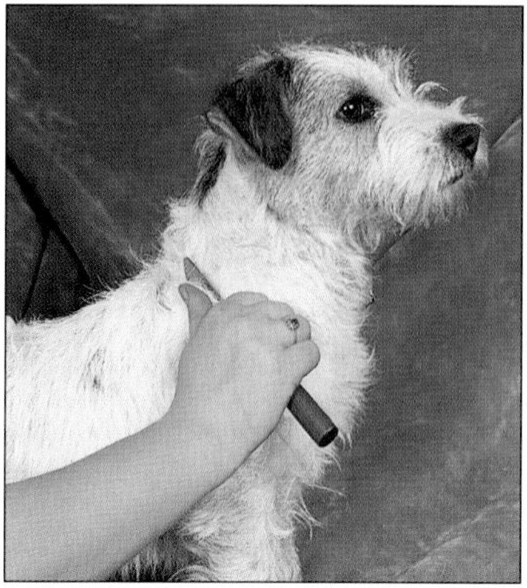

**You should start stripping your dog when he is still a puppy. If you accustom your Jack Russell to this procedure at an early age, he will better tolerate it as an older dog.**

dog's eyes whilst you are washing the rest of his body. Work the shampoo all the way down to the skin. You can use this opportunity to check the skin for any bumps, bites or other abnormalities. Do not neglect any area of the body—get all of the hard-to-reach places.

Once the dog has been thoroughly shampooed, he requires an equally thorough rinsing. Shampoo left in the coat can be irritating to the skin. Protect his eyes from the shampoo by shielding them with your hand and directing the flow of water in the opposite direction. You should also avoid getting water in the ear canal. Be prepared for your dog to shake out his coat—you might want to stand back, but make sure you have a hold on the dog to keep him from running through the house.

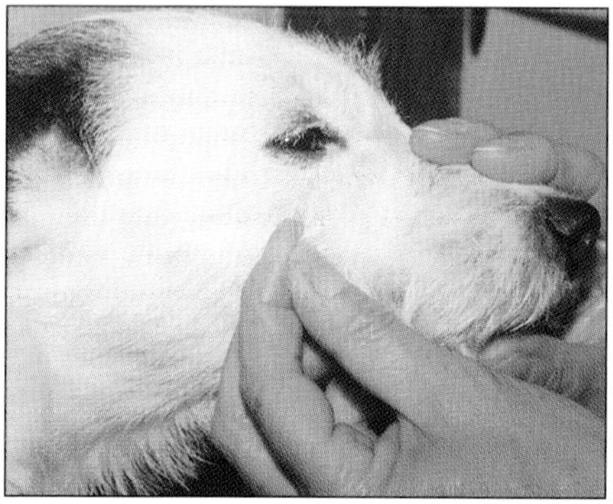

**Clean the tear stains around from your dog's eyes. Your local pet shop offers a special cleaner to assist in the process.**

## Did You Know?

The use of human soap products like shampoo, bubble bath and hand soap can be damaging to a dog's coat and skin. Human products are too strong and remove the protective oils coating the dog's hair and skin (making him water-resistant). Use only shampoo made especially for dogs and you may like to use a medicated shampoo, which will always help to keep external parasites at bay.

### Nail Clipping

Whether you are grooming a smooth coat or a rough coat, it is a good time to trim the nails on all four feet after removing your Jack Russell from the bath and towelling the coat. Return him to the grooming table to trim nails. He should become accustomed to the procedure at an early age, since it will be part of your maintenance routine throughout his life. Not only does it look nicer, but long nails can be sharp if they scratch someone unintentionally. Also, a long nail has a better chance of ripping and bleeding, or causing the feet to spread. A good rule of thumb is that if you can hear your dog's nails clicking on the floor when he walks, his nails are too long.

Before you start cutting, make sure you can identify the 'quick' in each nail. The quick is a blood vessel that runs through the centre of each nail and grows rather close to the end. It will bleed if accidentally cut, which will be quite painful for the dog as it contains nerve endings. Keep some type of clotting agent on hand, such as a styptic pencil or styptic powder (the type used for shaving). This will stop the bleeding quickly when applied to the end of the cut nail. Do not panic if you cut the quick, just stop the bleeding and talk soothingly to your dog. Once he has calmed down, move on to the next nail. It is better to clip a little at a time, particularly with black-nailed dogs.

## Grooming Tip

Once you are sure that the dog is thoroughly rinsed, squeeze the excess water out of the coat with your hand and dry him with a heavy towel. You may choose to use a blaster on his coat or just let it dry naturally. In cold weather, never allow your dog outside with a wet coat.

There are 'dry bath' products on the market, which are sprays and powders intended for spot cleaning, that can be used between regular baths, if necessary. They are not substitutes for regular baths, but they are easy to use for touch-ups as they do not require rinsing.

Hold your pup steady as you begin trimming his nails; you do not want him to make any sudden movements or run away. Talk to him soothingly and stroke him as you clip. Holding his foot in your hand, simply take off the end of each nail in one quick clip. You can purchase nail clippers that are specially made for dogs; you can probably find them wherever you buy pet or grooming supplies.

After trimming the nails, you can finish up by either drying your dog with a hair dryer and

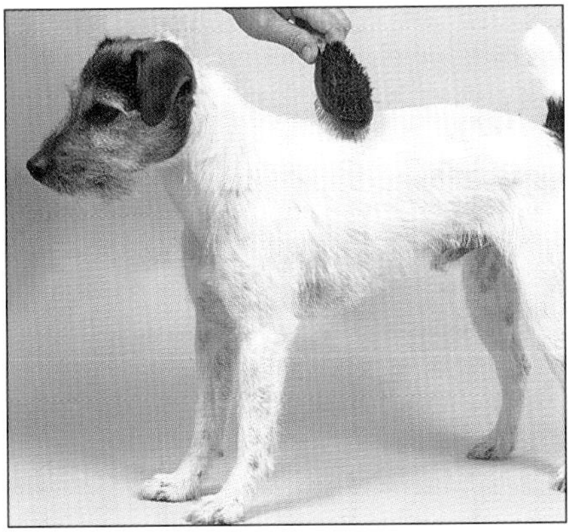

**Brushing is a normal, daily grooming chore to remove dead hairs. It will make your dog feel better and help keep your house neat.**

brushing him out again, or you can let him dry naturally and then brush him out. Dogs do not need to be bathed as often as humans, but regular bathing is essential for healthy skin and a healthy, shiny coat. Again, like most anything, if you accustom your pup to being bathed as a puppy, it will be second nature by the time he grows up. You want your dog to be at ease in the bath or else it could end up a wet, soapy, messy ordeal for both of you!

To conclude, your pet should be brushed weekly and bathed as needed. Trim the toenails and whiskers every month or so. Follow this plan and you will have a neat and clean Jack Russell that will be a crowd pleaser, whether in the show ring or in your home.

### Ear Cleaning

The ears should be kept clean and any excess hair inside the ear should be carefully plucked. Ears can be cleaned with a cotton wipe and special cleaner or ear powder made especially for dogs. Avoid probing into the dog's ear, as this can cause problems, and be very gentle and careful. Take the time to check for any signs of infection or ear mite infestation. If your Jack Russell has been shaking his head or scratching at his ears frequently, this usually indicates a problem. If his ears have an unusual odour, this is a

**Your dog's nails should be trimmed regularly. Clip only the bottom portion of the nail, avoiding the quick. If you cut into the quick, the nail will bleed and the dog will experience pain. A styptic pencil will stop the bleeding. Reassure the injured dog by talking quietly to him.**

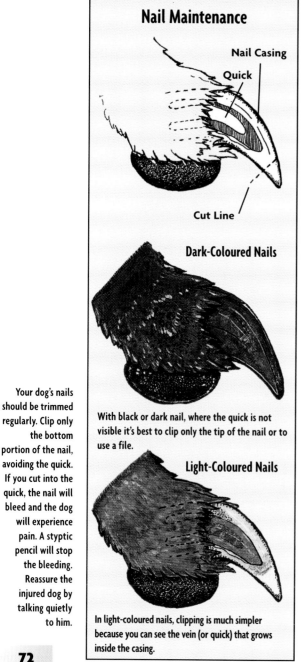

### Nail Maintenance

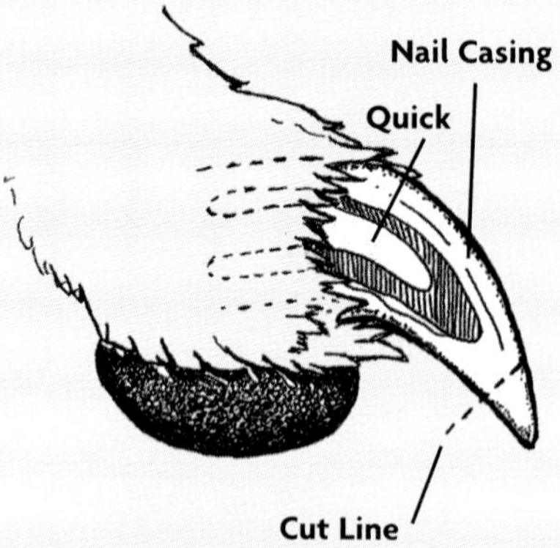


**Dark-Coloured Nails**

**With black or dark nail, where the quick is not visible it's best to clip only the tip of the nail or to use a file.**

**Light-Coloured Nails**

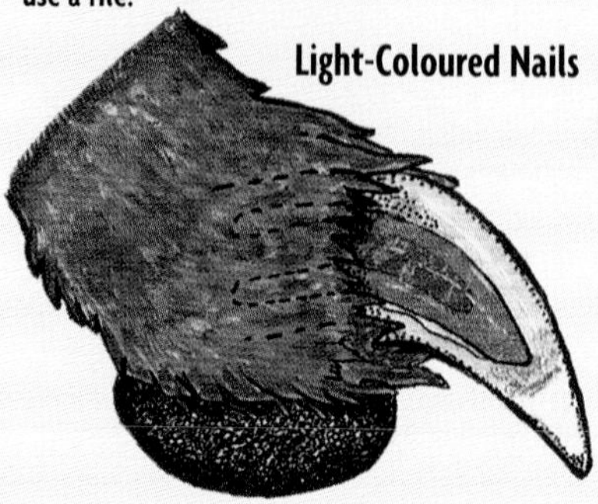

**In light-coloured nails, clipping is much simpler because you can see the vein (or quick) that grows inside the casing.**

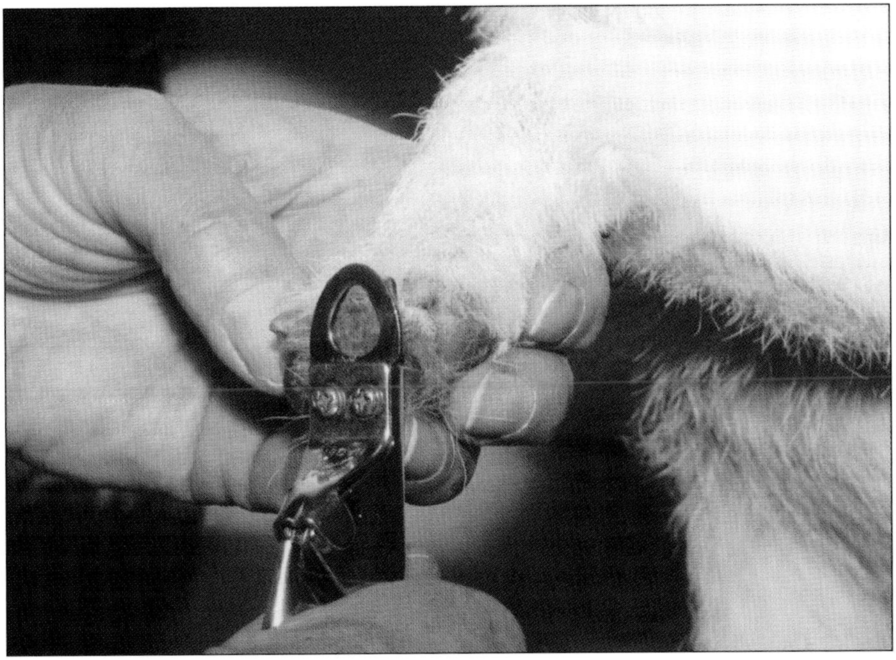

**Your local pet shop has special nail clippers to enable you to safely and painlessly cut your Jack Russell's toenails.**

sure sign of mite infestation or infection, and a signal to have his ears checked by the veterinary surgeon.

### TRAVELLING WITH YOUR DOG

#### Car Travel

You should accustom your Jack Russell to riding in a car at an early age. You may or may not take him in the car often, but at the very least he will need to go to the vet and you do not want these trips to be traumatic for the dog or a big hassle for you. The safest way for a dog to ride in the car is in his crate. If he uses a crate in the house, you can use the same crate for travel, if your vehicle can

## Did You Know?

When your dog spends a lot of time walking on a hard surface, such as cement or pavement, will have his nails naturally worn down and may not need to have them trimmed as often, except maybe in the colder months when he is not outside as much. Regardless, it is best to get your dog accustomed to this procedure at an early age so that he is used to it. Some dogs are especially sensitive about having their feet touched, but if a dog has experienced it since he was young, he should not be bothered by it.

Wherever you travel with your dog, his toilet relief schedule should not be altered. A suitable relief site should be visited at the proper time, and don't forget to clean up! This should be part of your travel plans.

These Jack Russells are curious to see where they're going, but it's much safer for them to enjoy the view from their crates. An open window is especially dangerous as the dogs can easily escape from the car.

accommodate it. Put the pup in the crate and see how he reacts. If the puppy seems uneasy, you can have a passenger hold him on his lap whilst you drive. Another option is a specially made safety harness for dogs, which straps the dog in much like a seat belt.

Do not let the dog roam loose in the vehicle—this is very dangerous! If you should stop short, your dog can be thrown and injured. If the dog starts climbing on you and pestering you whilst you are driving, you will not be able to concentrate on the road. It is an unsafe situation for everyone—human and canine.

For long trips, be prepared to stop to let the dog relieve himself.

Never drive with your Jack Russell loose within the car. A sudden turn or stop could cause injury to the dog and driver.

### Travel Tip

If you are going on a long motor trip with your dog, be sure the hotels are dog friendly. Many hotels do not accept dogs. Also take along some ice that can be thawed and offered to your dog if he becomes overheated. Most dogs like to lick ice.

Bring along whatever you need to clean up after him. You should take along some paper kitchen towels and perhaps some old towelling for use should he have an accident in the car or suffer from travel sickness.

#### Air Travel

Whilst it is possible to take a dog on a flight within Britain, this is fairly unusual and advance permission is always required. The dog will be required to travel in a fibreglass crate and you should always check in advance with the airline regarding specific requirements. To help the dog be at ease, put one of his favourite toys in the crate with him. Do not feed the dog for at least six hours before the trip to minimise his need to relieve himself. However, certain regulations specify that water must always be made available to the dog in the crate.

Make sure your dog is properly identified and that your

## Travel Tip

Never leave your dog alone in the car. In hot weather your dog can die from the high temperature inside a

closed vehicle; even a car parked in the shade can heat up very quickly. Leaving the window open is dangerous as well since the dog can hurt himself trying to get out.

contact information appears on his ID tags and on his crate. Animals travel in a different area of the plane than human passengers so every rule must be strictly adhered to so as to prevent the risk of getting separated from your dog.

**Boarding**

So you want to take a family holiday—and you want to include all members of the family. You would probably make arrangements for accommodations ahead of time anyway, but this is especially important when travelling with a dog. You do not want to make an overnight stop at the only place around for miles and find out that they do not allow dogs. Also, you do not want to reserve a place for your family without confirming that you are travelling with a dog because if it is against their policy you may not have a place to stay.

Alternatively, if you are travelling and choose not to bring your Jack Russell, you will have to make arrangements for him whilst you are away. Some options are to take him to a neighbour's house to stay whilst you are gone, to have a trusted neighbour pop in often or

## Travel Tip

When travelling, never let your dog off-lead in a strange area. Your dog could run away out of

fear or decide to chase a passing squirrel or cat or simply want to stretch his legs without restriction—you might never see your canine friend again.

Select a boarding kennel convenient to your home. The kennel should be neat, clean and spacious, and have a programme that will enable your dog to be exercised properly.

stay at your house, or bring your dog to a reputable boarding kennel. If you choose to board him at a kennel, you should visit in advance to see the facilities provided, how clean they are and where the dogs are kept. Talk to some of the employees and see how they treat the dogs—do they spend time with the dogs, play with them, exercise them, etc.? Also find out the kennel's policy on vaccinations and what they require. This is for all of the dogs' safety, since when dogs are kept together, there is a greater risk of diseases being passed from dog to dog.

## IDENTIFICATION

Your Jack Russell is your valued companion and friend. That is why you always keep a close eye on him and you have made sure that he cannot escape from the garden or wriggle out of his collar and run away from you. However, accidents can happen and there may come a time when your dog unexpectedly gets separated from you. If this unfortunate event should occur, the first thing on your mind will be finding him. Proper identification, including an ID tag, a tattoo and possibly a microchip, will increase the chances of his being returned to you safely and quickly.

## Did You Know?

If your dog gets lost, he is not able to ask for directions home.

Identification tags fastened to the collar give important information—the dog's name, the owner's name, the owner's address and a telephone number where the owner can be reached. This makes it easy for whom ever finds the dog to contact the owner and arrange to have the dog returned. An added advantage is that a person will be more likely to approach a lost dog who has ID tags on his collar; it tells the person that this is somebody's pet rather than a stray. This is the easiest and fastest method of identification provided that the tags stay on the collar and the collar stays on the dog.

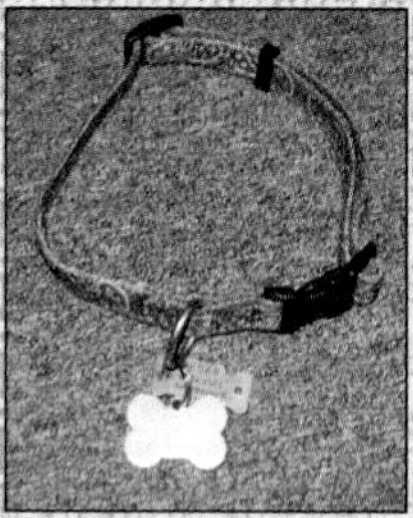

## Did You Know?

As puppies become more and more expensive, especially those puppies of high quality for showing and/or breeding, they have a greater chance of being stolen. The usual collar dog tag is, of course, easily removed. But there are two techniques that have become widely used for identification.

The puppy microchip implantation involves the injection of a small microchip, about the size of a corn kernel, under the skin of the dog. If your dog shows up at a clinic or shelter, or is offered for resale under less than savory circumstances, it can be positively identified by the microchip. The microchip is scanned and a registry quickly identifies you as the owner. This is not only protection against theft, but should the dog run away or go chasing a squirrel and get lost, you have a fair chance of getting it back.

Tattooing is done on various parts of the dog, from its belly to its cheeks. The number tattooed can be your telephone number or any other number which you can easily memorise. When professional dog thieves see a tattooed dog, they usually lose interest in it. Both microchipping and tattooing can be done at your local veterinary clinic. For the safety of our dogs, no laboratory facility or dog broker will accept a tattooed dog as stock.

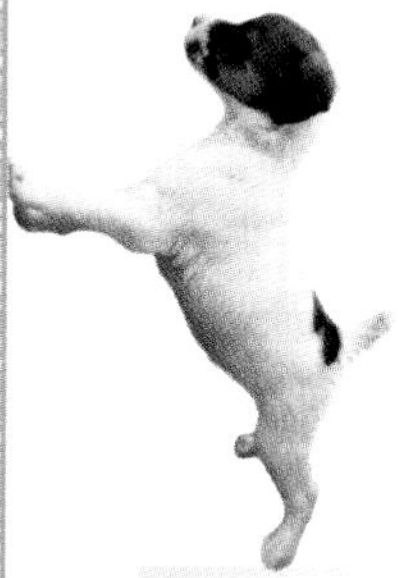

# HOUSEBREAKING AND TRAINING YOUR PARSON JACK RUSSELL TERRIER

Living with an untrained dog is a lot like owning a piano that you do not know how to play—it is a nice object to look at but it does not do much more than that to bring you pleasure. Now try taking piano lessons and suddenly the piano comes alive and brings forth magical sounds and rhythms that set your heart singing and your body swaying.

The same is true with your Parson Jack Russell Terrier. Any dog is a big responsibility and if not trained sensibly may develop unacceptable behaviour that annoys you or could even cause family friction.

To train your Jack Russell, you may like to enrol in an obedience class. Teach him good manners as you learn how and why he behaves the way he does. Find out how to communicate with your dog and how to recognise and understand his communications with you. Suddenly the dog takes on a new role in your life—he is clever, interesting, well behaved and fun to be with. He demonstrates his bond of devotion to you daily. In other words, your Jack Russell does wonders for your ego because he constantly reminds you that you are not only his leader, you are his hero!

Those involved with teaching dog obedience and counselling owners about their dogs' behaviour have discovered some interesting facts about dog ownership. For example, training dogs when they are puppies results in the highest rate of success in developing well-mannered and well-adjusted adult dogs. Training an older dog, from six months to six years of age, can

**Did You Know?**

You have a valuable dog. If the dog is lost or stolen, you would undoubtedly become extremely

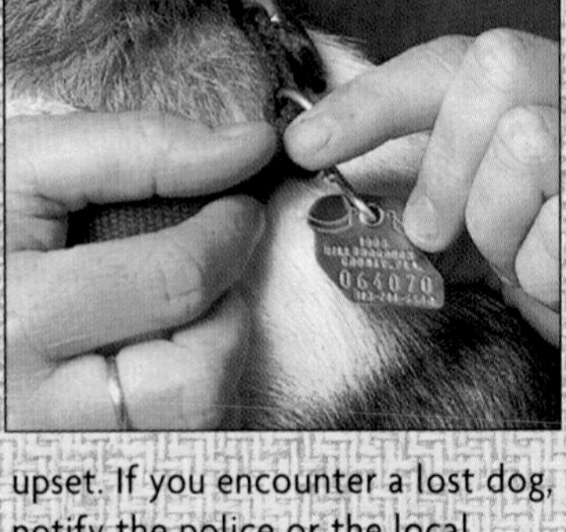

upset. If you encounter a lost dog, notify the police or the local animal shelter.

Proper training ensures that your Jack Russell pup will behave as sweetly as he looks.

produce almost equal results providing that the owner accepts the dog's slower rate of learning capability and is willing to work patiently to help the dog succeed at developing to his fullest potential. Unfortunately, many owners of untrained adult dogs lack the patience factor, so they do not persist until their dogs are successful at learning particular behaviours.

Training a puppy aged 10 to 16 weeks (20 weeks at the most) is like working with a dry sponge in a pool of water. The pup soaks up whatever you show him and constantly looks for more things to do and learn. At this early age, his body is not yet producing hormones, and therein lies the reason for such a high rate of success. Without hormones, he is focused on his owners and not particularly interested in investigating other places, dogs, people, etc. You are his leader: his provider of food, water, shelter and security. He latches onto you and wants to stay close. He will usually follow you from room to room, will not let you out of his sight when you are outdoors with him and will respond in like manner to the people and animals you encounter. If you greet a friend warmly, he will be happy to greet the person as well. If, however, you are hesitant, even anxious, about the approach of a stranger, he will respond accordingly.

Once the puppy begins to produce hormones, his natural curiosity emerges and he begins to

### Did You Know?

If you start with a normal, healthy dog and give him time, patience and some carefully executed lessons, you will reap the rewards of that training for the life of the dog. And what a life it will be! The two of you will find immeasurable pleasure in the companionship you have built together with love, respect and understanding.

investigate the world around him. It is at this time when you may notice that the untrained dog begins to wander away from you and even ignore your commands to stay close.

There are usually classes within a reasonable distance of the owner's home, but you also do a lot to train your dog yourself. Sometimes there are classes available but the tuition is too costly. Whatever the circumstances, the solution to the problem of lack of lesson availability lies within the pages of this book.

This chapter is devoted to helping you train your Jack Russell at home. If the recommended procedures are followed faithfully, you may expect positive results that will prove rewarding to both you and your dog.

Whether your new charge is a puppy or a mature adult, the methods of teaching and the techniques we use in training basic behaviours are the same. After all, no dog, whether puppy or adult, likes harsh or inhumane methods. All creatures, however, respond favourably to gentle motivational methods and sincere praise and encouragement. Now let us get started.

## Did You Know?

To a dog's way of thinking, your hands are like his mouth in terms of a defence mechanism. If you squeeze him too tightly, he might just bite you because that would be his normal response. This is not aggressive biting and, although all biting should be discouraged, you need the discipline in learning how to handle your dog.

## Training Tip

**Training a dog is a life experience. Many parents admit that much of what they know about raising children they learned from caring for their dogs. Dogs respond to love,**

**fairness and guidance, just as children do. Become a good dog owner and you may become an even better parent.**

**HOUSEBREAKING**

You can train a puppy to relieve itself wherever you choose, but this must be somewhere suitable. You should bear in mind from the outset that when your puppy is old enough to go out in public places, any canine deposits must be removed at once. You will

## Obedience School

A basic obedience beginner's class usually lasts for six to eight weeks. Dog and owner attend an hour-long lesson once a week and practise for a few minutes, several times a day, each day at home. If done properly, the whole procedure will result in a well-mannered dog and an owner who delights in living with a pet that is eager to please and enjoys doing things with his owner.

always have to carry with you a small plastic bag or 'poop-scoop.'

Outdoor training includes such surfaces as grass, soil and cement. Indoor training usually means training your dog to newspaper.

When deciding on the surface and location that you will want your Jack Russell to use, be sure it

is going to be permanent. Training your dog to grass and then changing your mind two months later is extremely difficult for both dog and owner.

Next, choose the command you will use each and every time you want your puppy to void. 'Hurry up' and 'Toilet' are examples of commands commonly used by dog owners.

Get in the habit of giving the puppy your chosen relief command before you take him out. That way, when he becomes an adult, you will be able to determine if he wants to go out when you ask him. A confirmation will be signs of interest, wagging his tail, watching you intently, going to the door, etc.

## Did You Know?

If you have other pets in the home and/or interact often with the pets of friends and

other family members, your pup will respond to those pets in much the same manner as you do. It is only when you show fear of or resentment toward another animal that he will act fearful or unfriendly.

**Always clean up after your dog whether your're in a public place or your own garden.**

Dogs have a ritual of sniffing out a suitable relief site before using it.

### Puppy's Needs

Puppy needs to relieve himself after play periods, after each meal, after he has been sleeping and any time he indicates that he is looking for a place to urinate or defecate.

The urinary and intestinal tract muscles of very young puppies are not fully developed. Therefore, like human babies, puppies need to relieve themselves frequently.

Take your puppy out often—every hour for an eight-week-old, for example, and always immediately after sleeping and eating. The older the puppy, the less often he will need to relieve himself. Finally, as a mature healthy adult, he will require only three to five relief trips per day.

### Housing

Since the types of housing and control you provide for your puppy have a direct relationship on the success of housetraining, we consider the various aspects of both before we begin training.

Bringing a new puppy home and turning him loose in your house can be compared to turning a child loose in a sports arena and telling the child that the place is all his! The sheer enormity of the place would be too much for him to handle.

Instead, offer the puppy clearly defined areas where he can

## Mealtime

Mealtime should be a peaceful time for your puppy. Do not put his food and water bowls in a high-traffic area in the house. For example, give him his own little

corner of the kitchen where he can eat undisturbed and where he will not be underfoot. Do not allow small children or other family members to disrupt the pup when he is eating.

play, sleep, eat and live. A room of the house where the family gathers is the most obvious choice. Puppies are social animals and need to feel a part of the pack right from the start. Hearing your voice, watching you whilst you are doing things and smelling you nearby are all positive reinforcers that he is now a member of your pack. Usually a family room, the kitchen or a nearby adjoining breakfast area is ideal for providing safety and security for both puppy and owner.

Within that room there should be a smaller area which the puppy can call his own. An alcove, a wire or fibreglass dog crate or a fenced (not boarded!) corner from which he can view the activities of his new family will be fine. The size of the area or crate is the key factor here. The area must be large enough for the puppy to lie down and stretch out as well as stand up without rubbing his head on the top, yet small enough so that he cannot relieve himself at one end and sleep at the other without coming into contact with his droppings until fully trained to relieve himself outside.

Dogs are, by nature, clean animals and will not remain close to their relief areas unless forced to do so. In those cases, they then become dirty dogs and usually remain that way for life.

The designated area should be lined with clean bedding and a toy. Water must always be available, in a non-spill container.

### Control

By control, we mean helping the puppy to create a lifestyle pattern that will be compatible to that of

**If you train your Jack Russell Terrier from puppyhood to accept the crate as his home, you will reap the benefits for his entire life.**

**If you have a crate, you can use it in the car for safety, as a home for your dog when staying in an unfamiliar location, or for ease of movement from one area of your house to another.**

Your Jack Russell Terrier should always sleep in his crate, but the crate need not always be closed. The puppy will learn to return to the crate on his own for sleep and solitude.

his human pack (YOU!). Just as we guide little children to learn our way of life, we must show the puppy when it is time to play, eat, sleep, exercise and even entertain himself.

Your puppy should always sleep in his crate. He should also learn that, during times of household confusion and excessive human activity such as at breakfast when family members are preparing for the day, he can play by himself in relative safety and comfort in his designated area. Each time you leave the puppy alone, he should understand exactly where he is to stay. You can gradually increase the time he is left alone to get him used to it. Puppies are chewers. They cannot tell the difference between lamp cords, television

## Did You Know?

Dogs will do anything for your attention. If you reward the dog when he is calm and resting, you will develop a well-mannered dog. If, on the other hand, you greet your dog excitedly and encourage him to wrestle and roughhouse with you, the dog will greet you the same way and you will have a hyper dog on your hands.

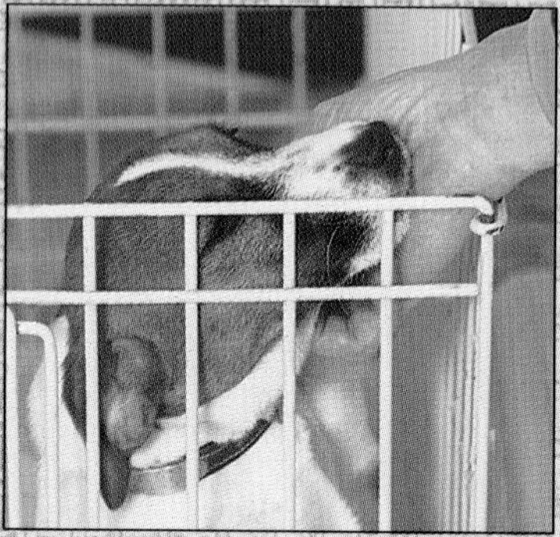

## Think Before You Bark!

Dogs are sensitive to their master's moods and emotions. Use your voice wisely when communicating with your dog. Never raise your voice at your dog unless you are angry and trying to correct him. 'Barking' at your dog can become as meaningless as 'dogspeak' is to you. Think before you bark!

wires, shoes, table legs, etc. Chewing into a television wire, for example, can be fatal to the puppy whilst a shorted wire can start a fire in the house.

If the puppy chews on the arm of the chair when he is alone, you will probably discipline him angrily when you get home. Thus, he makes the association that your coming home means he is going to be punished. (He will not remember chewing up the chair and is incapable of making the association of the discipline with his naughty deed.)

Other times of excitement, such as family parties, etc., can be fun for the puppy providing he can view the activities from the security of his designated area. He is not underfoot and he is not being fed all sorts of titbits that will probably cause him stomach distress, yet he still feels a part of the fun.

### Schedule

A puppy should be taken to his relief area each time he is released from his designated area, after meals, after a play session, when he first awakens in the morning (at age eight weeks, this can mean 5 a.m.!). The puppy will indicate that he's ready 'to go' by circling or sniffing busily—-do not misinterpret these signs. For a puppy less than ten weeks of age, a routine of taking him out every hour is necessary. As the puppy grows, he will be able to wait for longer periods of time.

Keep trips to his relief area short. Stay no more than five or six minutes and then return to the house. If he goes during that time, praise him lavishly

**Puppies always squat when they urinate, regardless of whether they are male or female.**

## Success Method

Success that comes by luck is usually short lived. Success that comes by well-thought-out proven methods is often more easily achieved and permanent. This is the Success Method. It is designed to give you, the puppy owner, a simple yet proven way to help your puppy develop clean living habits and a feeling of security in his new environment.

## Did You Know?

Never line your pup's sleeping area with newspaper. Puppy litters are usually raised on newspaper and, once in your home, the puppy will immediately associate newspaper

with voiding. Never put newspaper on any floor while housetraining, as this will only confuse the puppy. If you are paper-training him, use paper in his designated relief area ONLY. Finally, restrict water intake after evening meals. Offer a few licks at a time—never let a young puppy gulp water after meals.

and take him indoors immediately. If he does not, but he has an accident when you go back indoors, pick him up immediately, say 'No! No!' and return to his relief area. Wait a few minutes, then return to the house again. never hit a puppy or rub his face in urine or excrement when he has an accident!

Once indoors, put the puppy in his crate until you have had time to clean up his accident. Then release him to the family area and watch him more closely than before. Chances are, his accident was a result of your not picking up his signal or waiting too long before offering him the opportunity to relieve himself. Never hold a grudge against the puppy for accidents.

Let the puppy learn that going outdoors means it is time to relieve himself, not play. Once trained, he will be able to play

indoors and out and still differentiate between the times for play versus the times for relief.

Help him develop regular hours for naps, being alone, playing by himself and just resting, all in his crate. Encourage him to entertain himself whilst you are busy with your activities. Let him learn that having you near is comforting, but it is not your main purpose in life to provide him with undivided attention.

Male Jack Russells raise their legs even when they have no target!

## Did You Know?

Your dog is actually training you at the same time you are

training him. Dogs do things to get attention. They usually repeat whatever succeeds in getting your attention.

Each time you put a puppy in his own area, use the same command, whatever suits best. Soon, he will run to his crate or special area when he hears you say those words.

Crate training provides safety for you, the puppy and the home. It also provides the puppy with a feeling of security, and that helps the puppy achieve self-confidence and clean habits.

Remember that one of the primary ingredients in housetraining your puppy is control. Regardless of your lifestyle, there will always be occasions when you will need to have a place where your dog can stay and be happy and safe. Training is the answer for now and in the future.

In conclusion, a few key elements are really all you need for a successful housetraining method—consistency, frequency, praise, control and supervision. By following these procedures with a normal, healthy puppy, you and the puppy will soon be past the stage of 'accidents' and ready to move on to a full and rewarding life together.

## Training Tip

**Stand up straight and authoritatively when giving your dog commands. Do not issue commands when lying on the floor or lying on your back on the sofa. If you are on your hands and knees when you give a command, your dog will think you are positioning yourself to play.**

### ROLES OF DISCIPLINE, REWARD AND PUNISHMENT

Discipline, training one to act in accordance with rules, brings order to life. It is as simple as that. Without discipline, particularly in a group society, chaos reigns supreme and the group will eventually perish. Humans and canines are social animals and need some form of discipline in order to function effectively. They must procure food, protect their home base and their young and reproduce to keep the species going.

If there were no discipline in the lives of social animals, they would eventually die from starvation and/or predation by other stronger animals.

In the case of domestic canines, dogs need discipline in their lives in order to understand how their pack (you and other family members) functions and how they must act in order to survive.

A large humane society in a highly populated area recently surveyed dog owners regarding their satisfaction with their relationships with their dogs. People who had trained their dogs were 75% more satisfied with their pets than those who had never trained their dogs.

Dr. Edward Thorndike, a psychologist, established *Thorndike's Theory of Learning*, which states that a behaviour that results in a pleasant event tends to be repeated. A behaviour that results in an unpleasant event tends not to be repeated. It is this theory on which training methods are based today. For example, if you manipulate a dog to perform a specific behaviour and reward him for doing it, he is likely to do it again because he enjoyed the end result.

Occasionally, punishment, a

# CANINE DEVELOPMENT SCHEDULE

It is important to understand how and at what age a puppy develops into adulthood. If you are a puppy owner, consult the following Canine Development Schedule to determine the stage of development your puppy is currently experiencing. This knowledge will help you as you work with the puppy in the weeks and months ahead.

| Period | Age | Characteristics |
|---|---|---|
| First to Third | Birth to Seven Weeks | Puppy needs food, sleep and warmth, and responds to simple and gentle touching. Needs mother for security and disciplining. Needs littermates for learning and interacting with other dogs. Pup learns to function within a pack and learns pack order of dominance. Begins socialising with adults and children for short periods. Begins to become aware of its environment. |
| Fourth | Eight to Twelve Weeks | Brain is fully developed. Needs socialising with outside world. Remove from mother and littermates. Needs to change from canine pack to human pack. Human dominance necessary. Fear period occurs between 8 and 16 weeks. Avoid fright and pain. |
| Fifth | Thirteen to Sixteen Weeks | Training and formal obedience should begin. Less association with other dogs, more with people, places, situations. Period will pass easily if you remember this is pup's change-to-adolescence time. Be firm and fair. Flight instinct prominent. Permissiveness and over-disciplining can do permanent damage. Praise for good behaviour. |
| Juvenile | Four to Eight Months | Another fear period about 7 to 8 months of age. It passes quickly, but be cautious of fright and pain. Sexual maturity reached. Dominant traits established. Dog should understand sit, down, come and stay by now. |

Note: These are approximate time frames. Allow for individual differences in puppies.

penalty inflicted for an offence, is necessary. The best type of punishment often comes from an outside source. For example, a child is told not to touch the stove because he may get burned. He disobeys and touches the stove. In doing so, he receives a burn. From that time on, he respects the heat of the stove and avoids contact with it. Therefore, a behaviour that results in an unpleasant event tends not to be repeated.

A good example of a dog learning the hard way is the dog who chases the house cat. He is

## How Many Times a Day?

| AGE | RELIEF TRIPS |
|---|---|
| To 14 weeks | 10 |
| 14–22 weeks | 8 |
| 22–32 weeks | 6 |
| Adulthood (dog stops growing) | 4 |

These are estimates, of course, but they are a guide to the MINIMUM opportunities a dog should have each day to relieve itself.

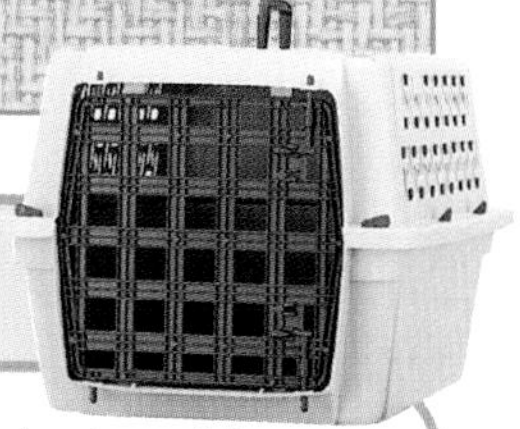

## THE SUCCESS METHOD

**1** Tell the puppy 'Crate time!' and place him in the crate with a small treat (a piece of cheese or half of a biscuit). Let him stay in the crate for five minutes while you are in the same room. Then release him and praise lavishly. Never release him when he is fussing. Wait until he is quiet before you let him out.

**2** Repeat Step 1 several times a day.

**3** The next day, place the puppy in the crate as before. Let him stay there for ten minutes. Do this several times.

**4** Continue building time in five-minute increments until the puppy stays in his crate for 30 minutes with you in the room. Always take him to his relief area after prolonged periods in his crate.

**5** Now go back to Step 1 and let the puppy stay in his crate for five minutes, this time while you are out of the room.

**6** Once again, build crate time in five-minute increments with you out of the room. When the puppy will stay willingly in his crate (he may even fall asleep!) for 30 minutes with you out of the room, he will be ready to stay in it for several hours at a time.

## *6 Steps to Successful Crate Training*

told many times to leave the cat alone, yet he persists in teasing the cat. Then, one day he begins chasing the cat but the cat turns and swipes a claw across the dog's face, leaving him with a painful gash on his nose. The final result is that the dog stops chasing the cat.

## TRAINING EQUIPMENT

### Collar and Lead

For a Jack Russell, the collar and lead that you use for training must be one with which you are easily able to work, not too heavy for the dog and perfectly safe.

Treats are a never-fail bribe. They are effective motivators in training, but keep in mind that you can't use treats forever and that your dog must learn to obey when not rewarded with food.

### Housebreaking Tip

Do not carry your dog to his toilet area. Lead him there on a leash or, better yet, encourage him to follow you to the spot. If you start carrying him to his spot, you might end up doing this routine forever and your dog will have the satisfaction of having trained YOU.

### Treats

Have a bag of treats on hand. Something nutritious and easy to swallow works best. Use a soft treat, a chunk of cheese or a piece of cooked chicken rather than a dry biscuit. By the time the dog has finished chewing a dry treat, he will forget why he is being rewarded in the first place! Using food rewards will not teach a dog to beg at the table—the only way to teach a dog to beg at the table is to give him food from the table. In training, rewarding the dog with a food treat will help him associate praise and the treats with learning new behaviours that obviously please his owner.

## TRAINING BEGINS: ASK THE DOG A QUESTION

In order to teach your dog anything, you must first get his attention. After all, he cannot learn anything if he is looking away from you with his mind on something else.

To get his attention, ask him, 'School?' and immediately walk over to him and give him a treat as you tell him 'Good dog.' Wait a minute or two and repeat the routine, this time with a treat in your hand as you approach within a foot of the dog. Do not go directly to him, but stop about a foot short of him and hold out the treat as you ask, 'School?' He will see you approaching with a treat in your hand and most likely begin walking toward you. As you meet, give him the treat and praise again.

The third time, ask the question, have a treat in your hand and walk only a short distance toward the dog so that he must walk almost all the way to you. As he reaches you, give him the treat and praise again.

By this time, the dog will probably be getting the idea that if he pays attention to you, especially when you ask that question, it will pay off in treats and fun activities for him. In other words, he learns that 'school' means doing fun things with you that result in treats and positive attention for him.

Remember that the dog does not understand your verbal language, he only recognises sounds. Your question translates to a series of sounds for him, and those sounds become the signal to

## Did You Know?

Dogs do not understand our language. They can be trained to react to a certain sound, at a certain volume. If you say 'No, Oliver' in a very soft pleasant voice it will not have the same meaning as 'No, Oliver!!' when you shout it as loud as you can. You should never use the dog's name during a reprimand, just the command NO!! Since dogs don't understand words, comics often use dogs trained with opposite meanings. Thus, when the comic commands his dog to SIT the dog will stand up, and vice versa.

## Practice Makes Perfect!

- Have training lessons with your dog every day in several short segments—three to five times a day for a few minutes at a time is ideal.
- Do not have long practice sessions. The dog will become easily bored.
- Never practise when you are tired, ill, worried or in an otherwise negative mood. This will transmit to the dog and may have an adverse effect on its performance.

Think fun, short and above all POSITIVE! End each session on a high note, rather than a failed exercise, and make sure to give a lot of praise. Enjoy the training and help your dog enjoy it, too.

go to you and pay attention; if he does, he will get to interact with you plus receive treats and praise.

## THE BASIC COMMANDS

### Teaching Sit

Now that you have the dog's attention, attach his lead and hold it in your left hand and a food treat in your right. Place your food hand at the dog's nose and let him lick the treat but not take it from you. Say 'Sit' and slowly raise your food hand from in front of the dog's nose up over his head so that he is looking at the ceiling. As he bends his head upward, he will have to bend his knees to maintain his balance. As he bends his knees, he will assume a sit position. At that point, release the food treat and praise lavishly with comments such as 'Good dog! Good sit!', etc. Remember to always praise enthusiastically, because dogs relish verbal praise from their owners and feel so proud of themselves whenever they accomplish a behaviour.

You will not use food forever in getting the dog to obey your commands. Food is only used to teach new behaviours, and once the dog knows what you want when you give a specific command, you will wean him off of the food treats but still maintain the verbal praise. After all, you will always have your voice with you, and there will be many times when you have no food rewards but expect the dog to obey.

## Housebreaking Tip

**Most of all, be consistent. Always take your dog to the same location, always use the same command, and always have him on lead when he is in his relief area, unless a fenced-in garden is available.**

**By following the Success Method, your puppy will be completely housetrained by the time his muscle and brain development reach maturity. Keep in mind that small breeds usually mature faster than large breeds, but all puppies should be trained by six months of age.**

## The Golden Rule

The golden rule of dog training is simple. For each 'question' (command), there is only one correct answer (reaction). One command = one reaction. Keep practising the command until the dog reacts correctly without hesitating. Be repetitive but not monotonous. Dogs get bored just as people do!

**Teaching Down**

Teaching the down exercise is easy when you understand how the dog perceives the down position, and it is very difficult when you do not. Dogs perceive the down position as a submissive one, therefore teaching the down exercise using a forceful method can sometimes make the dog develop such a fear of the down that he either runs away when you say 'Down' or he attempts to snap at the person who tries to force him down.

Have the dog sit close alongside your left leg, facing in the same direction as you are. Hold the lead in your left hand and a food treat in your right. Now place your left hand lightly on the top of the dog's shoulders where they meet above the spinal cord. Do not push down on the dog's shoulders; simply rest your left hand there so you can guide the dog to lie down close to your left leg rather than to swing away from your side when he drops.

**Teaching DOWN is a fairly easy exercise once you understand the dog's perspective on the exercise. Dogs consider DOWN as a submissive action.**

## Rules To Obey

If you want to be successful in training your dog, you have four rules to obey yourself:
1. Develop an understanding of how a dog thinks.
2. Do not blame the dog for lack of communication.
3. Define your dog's personality and act accordingly.
4. Have patience and be consistent.

## Training Tip

Never train your dog, puppy or adult, when you are mad or in a sour mood. Dogs are very sensitive to human feelings, especially anger, and if your dog senses that you are angry or upset, he will connect your anger with his training and learn to resent or fear his training sessions.

Now place the food hand at the dog's nose, say 'Down' very softly (almost a whisper), and slowly lower the food hand to the

dog's front feet. When the food hand reaches the floor, begin moving it forward along the floor in front of the dog. Keep talking softly to the dog, saying things like, 'Do you want this treat? You can do this, good dog.' Your reassuring tone of voice will help

## Did You Know?

Dogs are the most honourable animals in existence. They consider another species (humans) as their own. They interface with you. You are their leader. Puppies perceive children to be on their level; their actions around small children are different from their behaviour around their adult masters.

calm the dog as he tries to follow the food hand in order to get the treat.

When the dog's elbows touch the floor, release the food and praise softly. Try to get the dog to maintain that down position for several seconds before you let him sit up again. The goal here is to get the dog to settle down and not feel threatened in the down position.

## Did You Know?

A dog in jeopardy never lies down. He stays alert on his feet because instinct tells him that he may have to run away or fight for his survival. Therefore, if a dog feels threatened or anxious, he will not lie down. Consequently, it is important to have the dog calm and relaxed as he learns the down exercise.

## Information . . .

**The puppy should also have regular play and exercise sessions when he is with you or a family member.**

**Exercise for a very young puppy can consist of a short walk around the house or garden. Playing can include fetching games with a large ball or a special raggy. (All puppies teethe and need soft things upon which to chew.) Remember to restrict play periods to indoors within his living area (the family room, for example) until he is completely housetrained.**

### Teaching Stay

It is easy to teach the dog to stay in either a sit or a down position. Again, we use food and praise during the teaching process as we help the dog to understand exactly what it is that we are expecting him to do.

To teach the sit/stay, start with the dog sitting on your left side as before and hold the lead in your left hand. Have a food treat in your right hand and place your food hand at the dog's nose. Say 'Stay' and step

**You can teach your dog to STAY in either the SIT or the DOWN position.**

out on your right foot to stand directly in front of the dog, toe to toe, as he licks and nibbles the treat. Be sure to keep his head facing upward to maintain the sit position. Count to five and then swing around to stand next to the dog again with him on your left. As soon as you get back to the original position, release the food and praise lavishly.

## Information . . .

**Dogs are as different from each other as people are. What works for one dog may not work for another.**

**Have an open mind. If one method of training is unsuccessful, try another.**

To teach the down/stay, do the down as previously described. As soon as the dog lies down, say 'Stay' and step out on your right foot just as you did in the sit/stay. Count to five and then return to stand beside the dog with him on your left side. Release the treat and praise as always.

Within a week or ten days, you can begin to add a bit of distance between you and your dog when you leave him. When you do, use your left hand open with the palm facing the dog as a stay signal, much the same as the hand signal a police officer uses to stop traffic at an intersection. Hold the food treat in your right hand as before, but this time the food is not touching the dog's nose. He will watch the food hand and quickly learn that he is going to get that treat as soon as you return to his side.

When you can stand 1 metre away from your dog for 30 seconds, you can then begin building time and distance in both stays. Eventually, the dog can be expected to remain in the stay position for prolonged periods of time until you return to him or call him to you. Always praise lavishly when he stays.

### Teaching Come

If you make teaching 'come' a fun experience, you should never have a 'student' that does not love the game or that fails to come when called. The secret, it seems, is never to teach the word 'come.'

## Did You Know?

Never call your dog to come to you for a correction or scold him when he reaches you. That is the quickest way to turn a 'Come' command into 'Go away fast!' Dogs think only in the present tense, and your dog will connect the scolding with coming to you, not with the misbehaviour of a few moments earlier.

At times when an owner most wants his dog to come when called, the owner is likely to be upset or anxious and he allows these feelings to come through in the tone of his voice when he calls his dog. Hearing that desperation in his owner's voice, the dog fears the results of going to him and therefore either disobeys outright or runs in the opposite direction. The secret, therefore, is to teach the dog a game and, when you want him to come to you, simply play the game. It is practically a no-fail solution!

To begin, have several members of your family take a few food treats and each go into a different room in the house. Take turns calling the dog, and each person should celebrate the dog's finding him with a treat and lots of happy praise. When a person calls the dog, he is actually inviting the dog to find him and get a treat as a reward for 'winning.'

A few turns of the 'Where are you?' game and the dog will work out that everyone is playing the game and that each person has a big celebration awaiting his success at locating them. Once he learns to love the game, simply calling out 'Where are you?' will bring him running from wherever he is when he hears that all-important question.

The come command is recognised as one of the most

## Did You Know?

When calling the dog, do not say 'Come.' Say things like, 'Rover, where are you? See if you can find me! I have a biscuit for you!' Keep up a constant line of chatter with coaxing sounds and frequent questions such as, 'Where are you?' The dog will learn to follow the sound of your voice to locate you and receive his reward.

important things to teach a dog, but there are trainers who work with thousands of dogs and never teach the actual word 'Come.' Yet these dogs will race to respond to a person who uses the dog's name followed by 'Where are you?' For example, a woman has a 12-year-old companion dog who went blind, but who never fails to locate her owner when asked, 'Where are you?'

Children particularly love to play this game with their dogs. Children can hide in smaller places like a shower or bath, behind a bed or under a table. The dog needs to work a little bit harder to find these hiding places, but when he does he loves to celebrate with a treat and a tussle with a favourite youngster.

### Did You Know?

Play fetch games with your puppy in an enclosed area where he can retrieve his toy and bring it back

to you. Always use a toy or object designated just for this purpose. Never use a shoe, stocking or other item he may later confuse with those in your wardrobe or underneath your chair.

### Teaching Heel

Heeling means that the dog walks beside the owner without pulling. It takes time and patience on the owner's part to succeed at teaching the dog that he (the owner) will not proceed unless the dog is walking calmly beside him. Pulling out ahead on the lead is definitely not acceptable.

Begin with holding the lead in your left hand as the dog sits beside your left leg. Move the loop end of the lead to your right hand but keep your left hand short on the lead so it keeps the dog in close next to you.

Say 'Heel' and step forward on your left foot. Keep the dog close to you and take three steps. Stop and have the dog sit next to you in what we now call the 'heel position.' Praise verbally, but do not touch the dog. Hesitate a moment and begin again with 'Heel,' taking three steps and stopping, at which point the dog is told to sit again.

Your goal here is to have the dog walk those three steps without pulling on the lead. When he will walk calmly beside you for three steps without pulling, increase the number of steps you take to five. When he will walk politely beside you whilst you take five steps, you can increase the length of your walk to ten steps. Keep increasing the length of your stroll until the dog

## Did You Know?

If you are walking your dog and he suddenly stops and looks straight into your eyes, ignore him. Pull the leash and lead him into the direction you want to walk.

will walk quietly beside you without pulling as long as you want him to heel. When you stop heeling, indicate to the dog that the exercise is over by verbally praising as you pet him and say 'OK, good dog.' The 'OK' is used as a release word meaning that the exercise is finished and the dog is free to relax.

If you are dealing with a dog who insists on pulling you around, simply 'put on your brakes' and stand your ground until the dog realises that the two of you are not going anywhere until he is beside you and moving at your pace, not his. It may take some time just standing there to convince the dog that you are the leader and you will be the one to decide on the direction and speed of your travel.

Each time the dog looks up at you or slows down to give a slack lead between the two of you, quietly praise him and say, 'Good heel. Good dog.' Eventually, the dog will begin to respond and within a few days he will be walking politely beside you without pulling on the lead. At first, the training sessions should be kept short and very positive; soon the dog will be able to walk nicely with you for increasingly longer distances. Remember also to give the dog free time and the opportunity to run and play when you have finished heel practice.

**WEANING OFF FOOD IN TRAINING**

Food is used in training new behaviours. Once the dog understands what behaviour goes

## Training Tip

If you begin teaching the heel by taking long walks and letting the dog pull you along, he

misinterprets this action as an acceptable form of taking a walk. When you pull back on the lead to counteract his pulling, he reads that tug as a signal to pull even harder!

## Training Tip

Teach your dog to HEEL in an enclosed area. Once you think the dog will obey reliably and you want to attempt advanced obedience exercises such as off-lead heeling, test him in a fenced-in area so he cannot run away.

with a specific command, it is time to start weaning him off the food treats. At first, give a treat after each exercise. Then, start to give a treat only after every other exercise. Mix up the times when you offer a food reward and the times when you only offer praise so that the dog will never know when he is going to receive both food and praise and when he is going to receive only praise. This is called a variable ratio reward system and it proves successful because there is always the chance that the owner will produce a treat, so the dog never stops trying for that reward. No matter what, ALWAYS give verbal praise.

**OBEDIENCE CLASSES**

It is a good idea to enrol in an obedience class if one is available in your area. If yours is a show dog, ringcraft classes would be more appropriate. Many areas have dog clubs that offer basic obedience training as well as preparatory classes for obedience competition. There are also local dog trainers who offer similar classes.

At obedience trials, dogs can earn titles at various levels of competition. The beginning levels of competition include basic behaviours such as sit, down, heel, etc. The more advanced levels of competition include jumping, retrieving, scent discrimination and signal work. The advanced levels require a dog and owner to put a lot of time and effort into their

## Obedience School

Taking your dog to an obedience school may be the best investment in time and money you can

ever make. You will enjoy the benefits for the lifetime of your dog and you will have the opportunity to meet people with your similar expectations for companion dogs. It also provides a basis for participating in other dog activities.

training and the titles that can be earned at these levels of competition are very prestigious.

**OTHER ACTIVITIES FOR LIFE**

Whether a dog is trained in the structured environment of a class or alone with his owner at home, there are many activities that can bring fun and rewards to both owner and dog once they have mastered basic control.

Teaching the dog to help out around the home, in the garden or on the farm provides great satisfaction to both dog and owner. In addition, the dog's help makes life a little easier for his owner and raises his stature as a valued companion to his family. It helps give the dog a purpose by occupying his mind and providing an outlet for his energy.

Backpacking is an exciting and healthy activity that the dog can be taught without assistance from more than his owner. The exercise of walking and climbing is good for man and dog alike, and the bond that they develop together is priceless.

If you are interested in participating in organised competition with your Jack Russell, there are activities other than obedience in which you and your dog can become involved. Agility is a popular and fun sport where dogs run through an obstacle course that includes various jumps, tunnels and other exercises to test the dog's speed and coordination. The owners run through the course beside their dogs to give commands and to guide them through the course. Although competitive, the focus is on fun—it's fun to do, fun to watch and great exercise.

**Jack Russell Terriers can enjoy a variety of activities, including swimming.**

## Internal Organs with Skeletal Structure

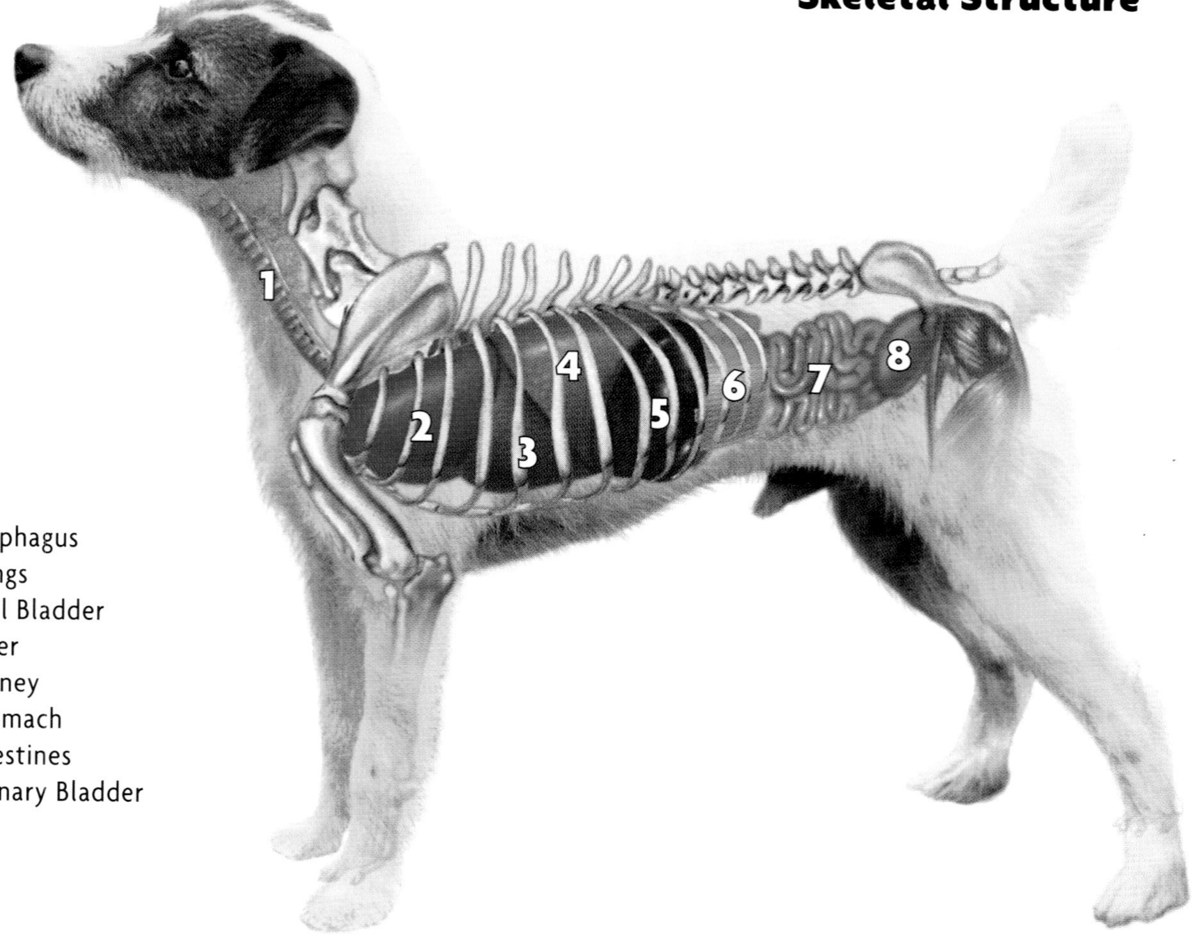


1. Esophagus
2. Lungs
3. Gall Bladder
4. Liver
5. Kidney
6. Stomach
7. Intestines
8. Urinary Bladder

# HEALTH CARE OF YOUR
# PARSON JACK RUSSELL TERRIER

Dogs suffer many of the same physical illnesses as people. They might even share many of the same psychological problems. Since people usually know more about human diseases than canine maladies, many of the terms used in this chapter will be familiar but not necessarily those used by veterinary surgeons. We will use the term *x-ray*, instead of the more acceptable term *radiograph*. We will also use the familiar term *symptoms* even though dogs don't have symptoms, which are verbal descriptions of the patient's feelings, dogs have *clinical signs*. Since dogs can't speak, we have to look for clinical signs...but we still use the term symptoms in this book.

As a general rule, medicine is practised. That term is not arbitrary. Medicine is a constantly changing art as we learn more and more about genetics, electronic aids (like CAT scans) and daily laboratory advances. There are many dog maladies, like canine hip dysplasia, which are not universally treated in the same manner. Some veterinary surgeons opt for surgery more often than others do.

## SELECTING A VETERINARY SURGEON

Your selection of a veterinary surgeon should not be based upon personality (as most are) but upon their convenience to your home. You want a vet who is close because you might have emergencies or need to make multiple visits for treatments. You want a vet who has services that you might require such as tattooing and grooming facilities, as well as sophisticated pet supplies and a good reputation for ability and responsiveness. There is nothing more frustrating than having to wait a day or more to get a response from your veterinary surgeon.

All veterinary surgeons are

**Your chosen veterinary surgeon should be familiar with the latest technologies and have all of the necessary equipment at his disposal.**

A typical American vet's income, categorised according to services provided. This survey dealt with small-animal practices.

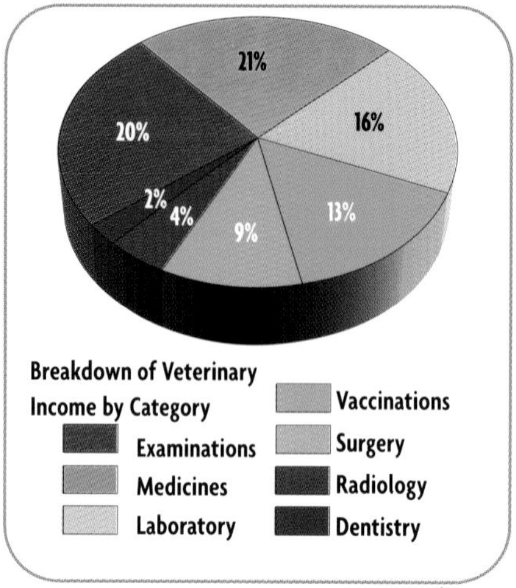


licensed and their diplomas and/or certificates should be displayed in their waiting rooms. There are, however, many veterinary specialities that usually require further studies and internships. There are specialists in heart problems (veterinary cardiologists), skin problems (veterinary dermatologists), teeth and gum problems (veterinary dentists), eye problems (veterinary ophthalmologists) and x-rays (veterinary radiologists), and surgeons who have specialities in bones, muscles or other organs. Most veterinary surgeons do routine surgery such as neutering, stitching up wounds and docking tails for those breeds in which such is required for show purposes. When the problem affecting your dog is serious, it is not unusual or impudent to get another medical opinion, although in Britain you are obliged to advise the vets concerned about this. You might also want to compare costs amongst several veterinary surgeons. Sophisticated health care and veterinary services can be very costly. Don't be bashful about discussing these costs with your veterinary surgeon or his (her) staff. It is not infrequent that important decisions are based upon financial considerations.

**PREVENTATIVE MEDICINE**

It is much easier, less costly and more effective to practise preventative medicine than to fight bouts of illness and disease. Properly bred puppies come from parents that were selected based upon their genetic disease profile. Their mothers should have been vaccinated, free of all internal and external parasites and properly nourished. For these reasons, a visit to the veterinary surgeon who cared for the dam (mother) is recommended. The dam can pass

**Did You Know?**

Male dogs are neutered. The operation removes the testicles and requires that the dog be anaesthetised. Recovery takes about one week. Females are spayed. This is major surgery and it usually takes a bitch two weeks to recover.

# First Aid at a Glance

**Burns**
Place the affected area under cool water; use ice if only a small area is burnt.

**Bee/Insect bites**
Apply ice to relieve swelling; antihistamine dosed properly.

**Animal bites**
Clean any bleeding area; apply pressure until bleeding subsides; go to the vet.

**Spider bites**
Use cold compress and a pressurised pack to inhibit venom's spreading.

**Antifreeze poisoning**
Immediately induce vomiting by using hydrogen peroxide.

**Fish hooks**
Removal best handled by vet; hook must be cut in order to remove.

**Snake bites**
Pack ice around bite; contact vet quickly; identify snake for proper antivenin.

**Car accident**
Move dog from roadway with blanket; seek veterinary aid.

**Shock**
Calm the dog, keep him warm; seek immediate veterinary help.

**Nosebleed**
Apply cold compress to the nose; apply pressure to any visible abrasion.

**Bleeding**
Apply pressure above the area; treat wound by applying a cotton pack.

**Heat stroke**
Submerge dog in cold bath; cool down with fresh air and water; go to the vet.

**Frostbite/Hypothermia**
Warm the dog with a warm bath, electric blankets or hot water bottles.

**Abrasions**
Clean the wound and wash out thoroughly with fresh water; apply antiseptic.

!! *Remember: an injured dog may attempt to bite a helping hand from fear and confusion. Always muzzle the dog before trying to offer assistance.* !!

on disease resistance to her puppies, which can last for eight to ten weeks. She can also pass on parasites and many infections. That's why you should visit the veterinary surgeon who cared for the dam.

**Weaning to Five Months Old**
Puppies should be weaned by the time they are about two months old. A puppy that remains for at least eight weeks with its mother and littermates usually adapts better to other dogs and people later in its life.

Some new owners have their puppy examined by a veterinary surgeon immediately, which is a good idea. Vaccination programmes usually begin when the puppy is very young.

The puppy will have its teeth examined and have its skeletal conformation and general health checked prior to certification by the veterinary surgeon. Puppies in certain breeds have problems with their kneecaps, eye cataracts and other eye problems, heart murmurs and undescended testicles. They may also have personality problems and your veterinary surgeon might have training in temperament evaluation.

### More Than Vaccines

Vaccinations help prevent your new puppy from contracting diseases, but they do not cure them. Proper nutrition as well as parasite control keep your dog healthy and less susceptible to many dangerous diseases. Remember that your dog depends on you to ensure his well being.

### Did You Know?

Cases of hyperactive adrenal glands (Cushing's disease) have been traced to the drinking of highly chlorinated water. Aerate or age your dog's drinking water before offering it.

**Vaccination Scheduling**
Most vaccinations are given by injection and should only be done by a veterinary surgeon. Both he and you should keep a record of the date of the injection, the identification of the vaccine and the amount given. Some vets give a first vaccination at eight weeks, but most dog breeders prefer the course not to commence until about ten weeks because of negating any antibodies passed on

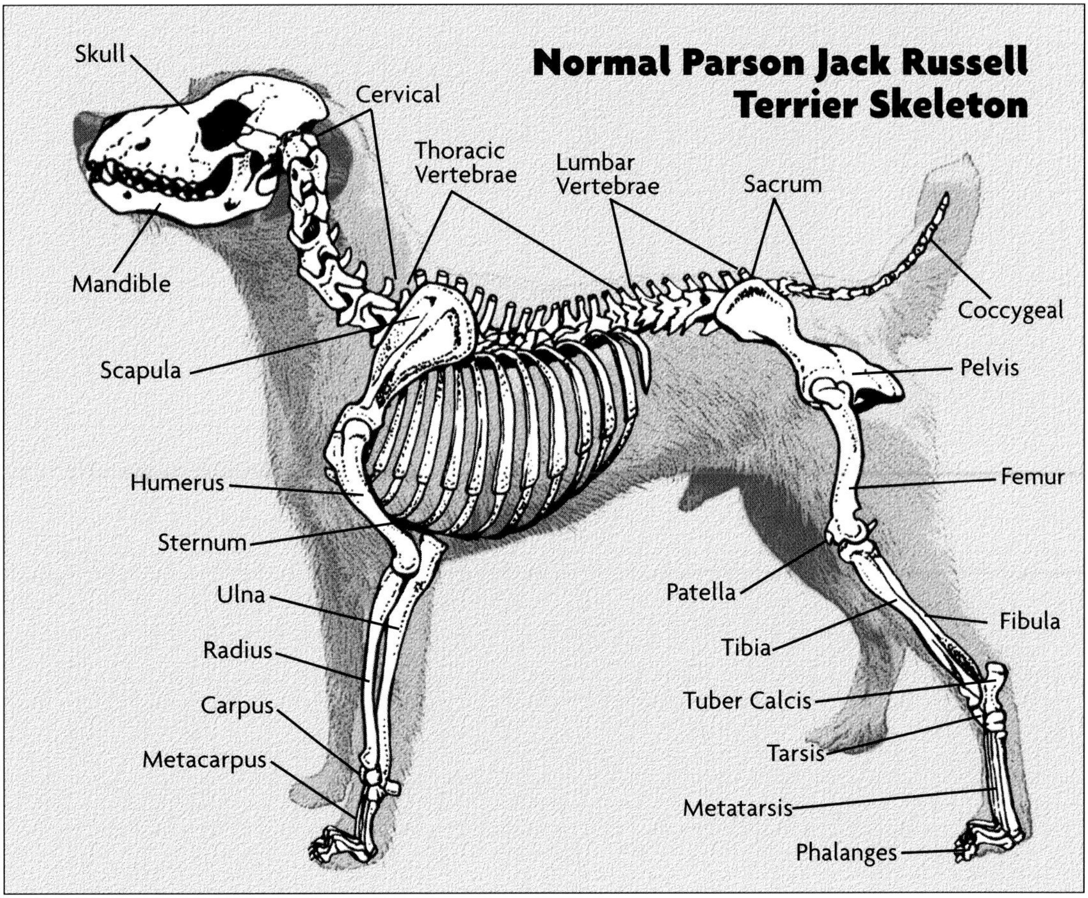


by the dam. The vaccination scheduling is usually based on a 15-day cycle. You must take your vet's advice as to when to vaccinate as this may differ according to the vaccine used. Most vaccinations immunise your puppy against viruses.

The usual vaccines contain immunising doses of several different viruses such as distemper, parvovirus, parainfluenza and hepatitis. There are other vaccines available when the puppy is at risk. You should rely upon professional advice. This is especially true for the booster-shot

## Did You Know?

Not every dog's ears are the same. Ears that are open to the air are healthier than ears with poor air circulation. Sometimes a dog can have two differently shaped ears. You should not probe inside your dog's ears. Only clean that which is accessible with a soft cotton wipe.

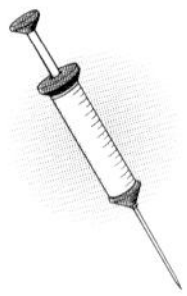

## HEALTH AND VACCINATION SCHEDULE

| Age in Weeks: | 3rd | 6th | 8th | 10th | 12th | 14th | 16th | 20-24th |
|---|---|---|---|---|---|---|---|---|
| Worm Control | ✔ | ✔ | ✔ | ✔ | ✔ | ✔ | ✔ | ✔ |
| Neutering | | | | | | | | ✔ |
| Heartworm* | | ✔ | | | | | | ✔ |
| Parvovirus | | ✔ | | ✔ | | ✔ | | ✔ |
| Distemper | | | ✔ | | ✔ | | ✔ | |
| Hepatitis | | | ✔ | | ✔ | | ✔ | |
| Leptospirosis | | ✔ | | ✔ | | ✔ | | |
| Parainfluenza | | ✔ | | ✔ | | ✔ | | |
| Dental Examination | | | ✔ | | | | | ✔ |
| Complete Physical | | | ✔ | | | | | ✔ |
| Temperament Testing | | | ✔ | | | | | |
| Coronavirus | | | | | ✔ | | | |
| Canine Cough | | ✔ | | | | | | |
| Hip Dysplasia | | | | | | | ✔ | |
| Rabies* | | | | | | | | ✔ |

Vaccinations are not instantly effective. It takes about two weeks for the dog's immunisation system to develop antibodies. Most vaccinations require annual booster shots. Your veterinary surgeon should guide you in this regard.

*Not applicable in the United Kingdom

programme. Most vaccination programmes require a booster when the puppy is a year old and once a year thereafter. In some cases, circumstances may require more frequent immunisations.

Kennel cough, more formally known as tracheobronchitis, is treated with a vaccine that is sprayed into the dog's nostrils. Kennel cough is usually included in routine vaccination, but this is often not so effective as for other major diseases.

### Five Months to One Year of Age

Unless you intend to breed or show your dog, neutering the puppy at

### Did You Know?

Vaccines do not work all the time. Sometimes dogs are allergic to them and many times the antibodies, which are supposed to be stimulated by the vaccine, just are not produced. You should keep your dog in the veterinary clinic for an hour after it is vaccinated to be sure there are no allergic reactions.

## Did You Know?

Your veterinary surgeon will probably recommend that your puppy be vaccinated before you take him outside. There are airborne diseases, parasite eggs in the grass and unexpected visits from other dogs that might be dangerous to your puppy's health.

six months of age is recommended. Discuss this with your veterinary surgeon; most professionals advise

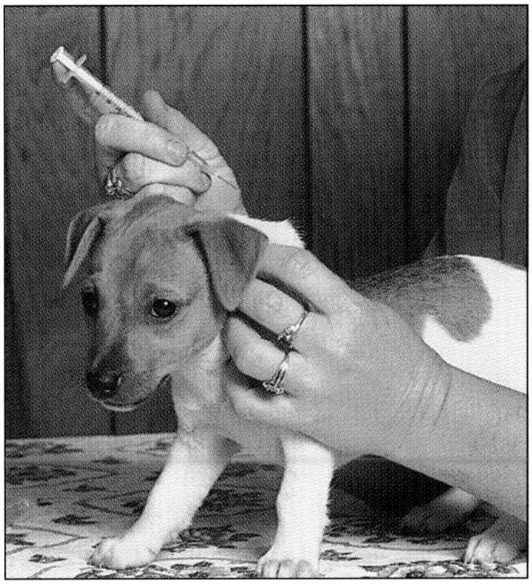

**The puppy's vaccination schedule should be complete by around 12-14 weeks of age.**

## DISEASE REFERENCE CHART

| | What is it? | What causes it? | Symptoms |
|---|---|---|---|
| **Leptospirosis** | Severe disease that affects the internal organs; can be spread to people. | A bacterium, which is often carried by rodents, that enters through mucous membranes and spreads quickly throughout the body. | Range from fever, vomiting and loss of appetite in less severe cases to shock, irreversible kidney damage and possibly death in most severe cases. |
| **Rabies** | Potentially deadly virus that infects warm-blooded mammals. Not seen in United Kingdom. | Bite from a carrier of the virus, mainly wild animals. | 1st stage: dog exhibits change in behaviour, fear.<br>2nd stage: dog's behaviour becomes more aggressive.<br>3rd stage: loss of coordination, trouble with bodily functions. |
| **Parvovirus** | Highly contagious virus, potentially deadly. | Ingestion of the virus, which is usually spread through the faeces of infected dogs. | Most common: severe diarrhoea.<br>Also vomiting, fatigue, lack of appetite. |
| **Kennel cough** | Contagious respiratory infection. | Combination of types of bacteria and virus.<br>Most common: *Bordetella bronchiseptica* bacteria and parainfluenza virus. | Chronic cough. |
| **Distemper** | Disease primarily affecting respiratory and nervous system. | Virus that is related to the human measles virus. | Mild symptoms such as fever, lack of appetite and mucous secretion progress to evidence of brain damage, 'hard pad.' |
| **Hepatitis** | Virus primarily affecting the liver. | Canine adenovirus type I (CAV-1). Enters system when dog breathes in particles. | Lesser symptoms include listlessness, diarrhoea, vomiting. More severe symptoms include 'blue-eye' (clumps of virus in eye). |
| **Coronavirus** | Virus resulting in digestive problems. | Virus is spread through infected dog's faeces. | Stomach upset evidenced by lack of appetite, vomiting, diarrhoea. |

neutering the puppy. Neutering has proven to be extremely beneficial to both male and female puppies. Besides eliminating the possibility of pregnancy, it inhibits (but does not prevent) breast cancer in bitches and prostate cancer in male dogs. It is very rare to diagnose breast cancer in a female dog who was spayed at or before about nine months of age before their first heat.

## Information . . .

**A dental examination is in order when the dog is between six months and one year of age so any permanent teeth that have erupted incorrectly can be corrected. It is important to begin a brushing routine, preferably using a two-sided brushing technique,**

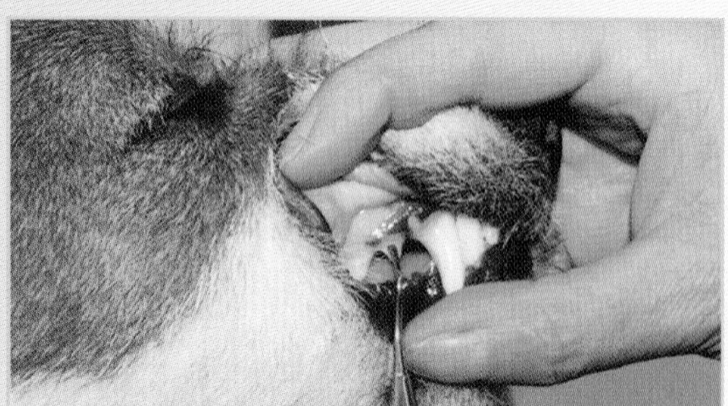

**whereby both sides of the tooth are brushed at the same time. Durable nylon and safe edible chews should be a part of your puppy's arsenal for good health, good teeth and pleasant breath. The vast majority of dogs three to four years old and older has diseases of the gums from lack of dental attention. Using the various types of dental chews can be very effective in controlling dental plaque.**

### Dogs Older Than One Year

Continue to visit the veterinary surgeon at least once a year. There is no such disease as old age, but bodily functions do change with age. The eyes and ears are no longer as efficient. Liver, kidney and intestinal functions often decline. Proper dietary changes, recommended by your veterinary surgeon, can make life more pleasant for the ageing Jack Russell and you.

## SKIN PROBLEMS IN JACK RUSSELLS

Veterinary surgeons are consulted by dog owners for skin problems more than any other group of diseases or maladies. Dogs' skin is almost as sensitive as human skin and both suffer almost the same ailments (though the occurrence of acne in dogs is rare!). For this reason, veterinary dermatology has developed into a speciality practised by many veterinary surgeons.

Since many skin problems have visual symptoms that are almost identical, it requires the skill of an experienced veterinary dermatologist to identify and cure many of the more severe skin disorders. Pet shops sell many treatments for skin problems but most of the treatments are directed at symptoms and not the underlying problem(s). If your dog is suffering from a skin disorder, you should seek professional assistance as quickly as possible. As with all diseases, the earlier a problem is identified and treated, the more successful is the cure.

**Inherited Skin Problems**

Many skin disorders are inherited and some are fatal. For example, acrodermatitis is an inherited disease that is transmitted by both parents. The parents, who appear (phenotypically) normal, have a recessive gene for acrodermatitis, meaning that they carry, but are not affected by, the disease.

Acrodermatitis is just one

## Acrodermatitis

There is a 25% chance of a puppy getting this fatal gene combination from two parents with recessive genes for acrodermatitis:

AA= NORMAL, HEALTHY
aa= FATAL
Aa= RECESSIVE, NORMAL APPEARING

If the female parent has an Aa gene and the male parent has an Aa gene, the chances are one in four that the puppy will have the fatal genetic combination aa.

**Dam** ♀ / **Sire** ♂

| Sire \ Dam | A | a |
|---|---|---|
| A | AA | Aa |
| a | Aa | aa |

## Did You Know?

It was announced in April 1999 that the severe quarantine laws imposed on animals entering Britain from other rabies-free countries would become a thing of the past by April 2001. Rather than being confined to a kennel for six months upon arrival in Britain, animals undergo a series of blood tests and vaccinations, and are identifed by microchip implantation. Qualified pets receive a 'health passport'

that allows their owners to travel with them in between Britain and other (mostly European) countries in which rabies does not exist.

Animals from countries such as the United States and Canada, where rabies is a problem, still will be subject to quarantine. Although veterinary standards are high in these countries, recently infected dogs may test negative to the disease and, without the quarantine period, may unknowingly introduce rabies into previously unaffected countries.

example of how difficult it is to prevent congenital dog diseases. The cost and skills required to ascertain whether two dogs should be mated are too high even though puppies with acrodermatitis rarely reach two years of age.

Other inherited skin problems are usually not as fatal as acrodermatitis. All inherited diseases must be diagnosed and treated by a veterinary specialist. There are active programmes being undertaken by many veterinary pharmaceutical manufacturers to solve most, if not all, of the common skin problems of dogs.

#### Parasite Bites

Many of us are allergic to insect bites. The bites itch, erupt and may even become infected. Dogs have the same reaction to fleas, ticks and/or mites. When an insect lands on you, you have the chance to whisk it away with your hand. Unfortunately, when your dog is bitten by a flea, tick or mite, it can only scratch it away or bite it. By the time the dog has been bitten, the parasite has done some of its damage. It may also have laid eggs to cause further problems in the near future. The itching from parasite bites is probably due to the saliva injected into the site when the parasite sucks the dog's blood.

#### Auto-Immune Skin Conditions

Auto-immune skin conditions are commonly referred to as being allergic to yourself, whilst allergies are usually inflammatory reactions to an outside stimulus. Auto-immune diseases cause serious damage to the tissues that are involved.

The best known auto-immune disease is lupus, which affects people as well as dogs. The symptoms are variable and may affect the kidneys, bones, blood chemistry and skin. It can be fatal to both dogs and humans, though it is not thought to be transmissible. It is usually successfully treated with cortisone, prednisone or similar corticosteroid, but extensive use of these drugs can have harmful side effects.

#### Airborne Allergies

An interesting allergy is pollen allergy. Humans have hay fever, rose fever and other fevers with which they suffer during the pollinating season. Many dogs suffer the same allergies. When the pollen count is high, your dog might suffer but don't expect him to sneeze and have a runny nose like humans. Dogs react to pollen allergies the same way they react to fleas—they scratch and bite themselves.

Dogs, like humans, can be tested for allergens. Discuss the testing with your veterinary dermatologist.

### FOOD PROBLEMS

#### Food Allergies

Dogs are allergic to many foods that are best-sellers and highly recommended by breeders and veterinary surgeons. Changing the brand of food that you buy may not eliminate the problem if the element to which the dog is allergic is contained in the new brand.

Recognising a food allergy is difficult. Humans vomit or have rashes when they eat a food to which they are allergic. Dogs neither vomit nor (usually) develop a rash. They react in the same manner as they do to an airborne or flea allergy: they itch, scratch and bite, thus making the diagnosis extremely difficult. Whilst pollen allergies and parasite bites are usually seasonal, food allergies are year-round problems.

### Food Intolerance

Food intolerance is the inability of the dog to completely digest certain foods. Puppies that may have done very well on their mother's milk may not do well on cow's milk. The result of this food intolerance may be loose bowels, passing gas and stomach pains. These are the only obvious symptoms of food intolerance and that makes diagnosis difficult.

### Treating Food Problems

It is possible to handle food allergies and food intolerance yourself. Put your dog on a diet that it has never had. Obviously if it has never eaten this new food it can't have been allergic or intolerant of it. Start with a single ingredient that is not in the dog's diet at the present time. Ingredients like chopped beef or fish are common in dogs' diets, so try something more exotic like rabbit, pheasant or even just vegetables. Keep the dog on this diet (with no additives) for a month. If the symptoms of food allergy or intolerance disappear, chances are your dog has a food allergy.

Don't think that the single ingredient cured the problem. You still must find a suitable diet and ascertain which ingredient in the old diet was objectionable. This is most easily done by adding ingredients to the new diet one at a time. Let the dog stay on the modified diet for a month before you add another ingredient. Eventually, you will determine the ingredient that caused the adverse reaction.

An alternative method is to carefully study the ingredients in the diet to which your dog is allergic or intolerant. Identify the main ingredient in this diet and eliminate the main ingredient by buying a different food that does not have that ingredient. Keep experimenting until the symptoms disappear after one month on the new diet.

**Did You Know?**

Never allow your dog to swim in polluted water or public areas where water quality can be suspect. Even perfectly clear water can harbour parasites, many of which can cause serious to fatal illnesses in canines. Areas inhabited by waterfowl and other wildlife are especially dangerous.

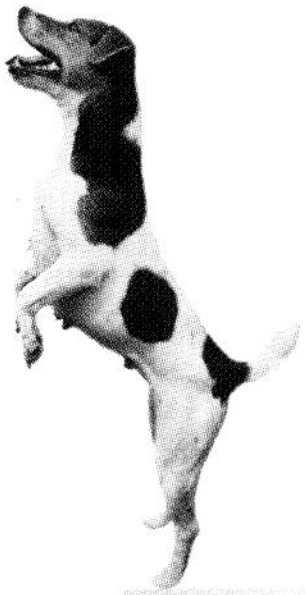

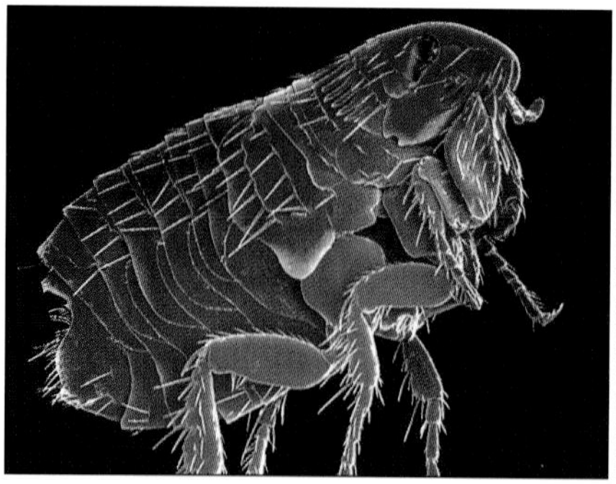
S. E. M. by Dr Dennis Kunkel, University of Hawaii

A scanning electron micrograph (S. E. M.) of a dog flea, *Ctenocephalides canis.*

Opposite page: A scanning electron micrograph of a dog or cat flea, *Ctenocephalides,* magnified more than 100x. This image has been colourized for effect.

## EXTERNAL PARASITES

Of all the problems to which dogs are prone, none is more well known and frustrating than fleas. Flea infestation is relatively simple to cure but difficult to prevent. Parasites that are harboured inside the body are a bit more difficult to eradicate but they are easier to control.

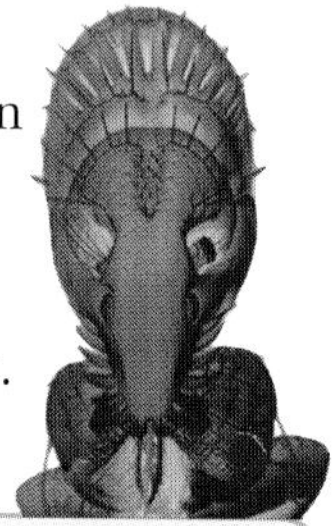

### Did You Know?

Fleas have been around for millions of years and have adapted to changing host animals.

They are able to go through a complete life cycle in less than one month or they can extend their lives to almost two years by remaining as pupae or cocoons. They do not need blood or any other food for up to 20 months.

They have been measured as being able to jump 300,000 times and can jump 150 times their length in any direction including straight up. Those are just a few of the reasons they are so successful in infesting a dog!

### Fleas

To control a flea infestation you have to understand the flea's life cycle. Fleas are often thought of as a summertime problem but centrally heated homes have changed the patterns and fleas can be found at any time of the year. The most effective method of flea control is a two-stage approach: one stage to kill the adult fleas, and the other to control the development of pre-adult fleas. Unfortunately, no single active ingredient is effective against all stages of the life cycle.

### Life Cycle Stages

During its life, a flea will pass through four life stages: egg, larva, pupa and adult. The adult stage is the most visible and irritating stage of the flea life

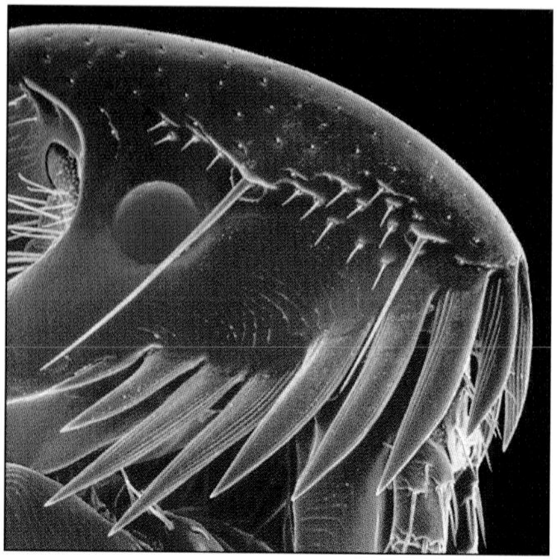
S. E. M. by Dr Dennis Kunkel, University of Hawaii

S. E. M. by Dr Dennis Kunkel, University of Hawaii

Magnified head of a dog flea, *Ctenocephalides canis.*

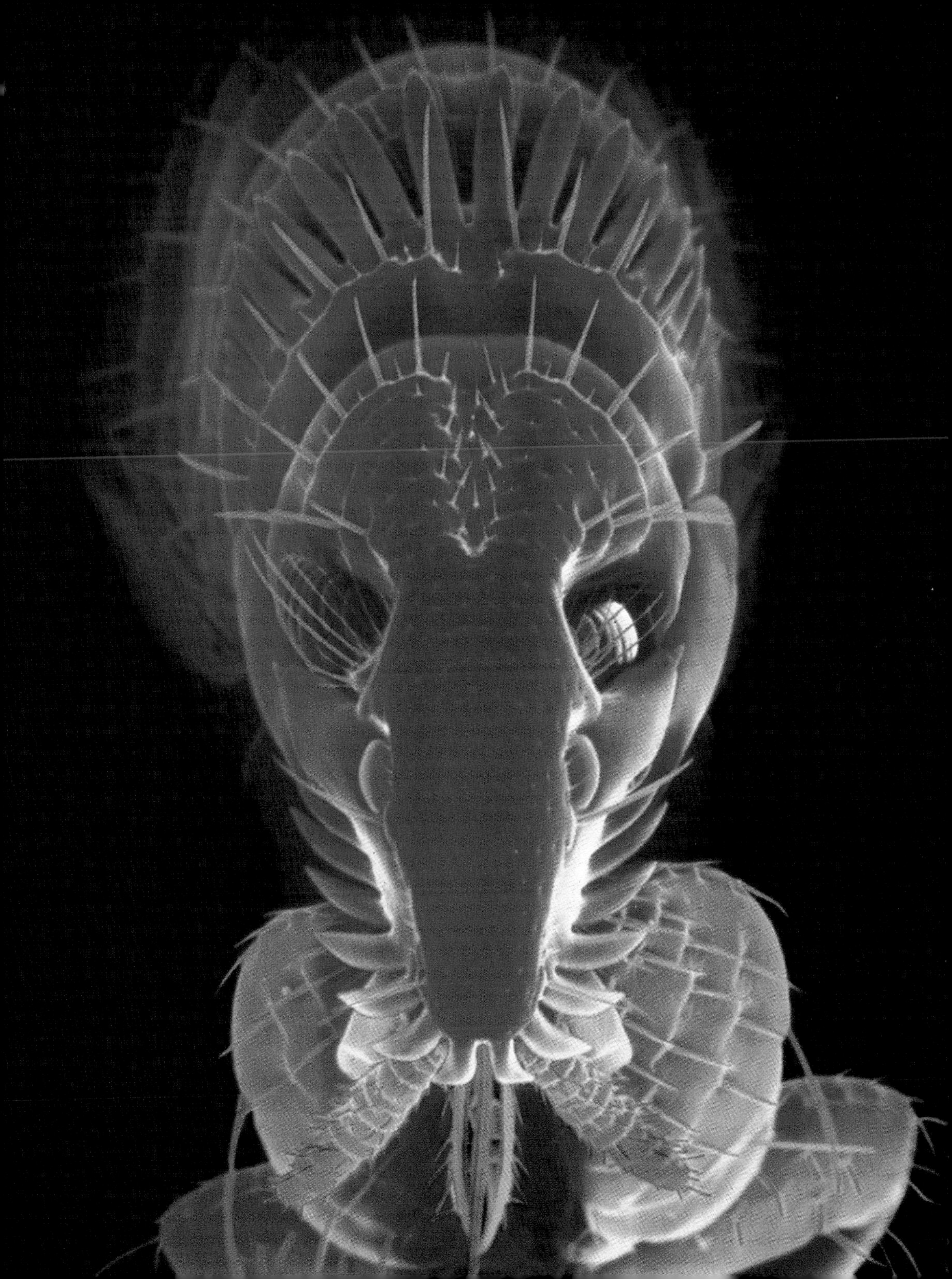

# The Life Cycle of the Flea

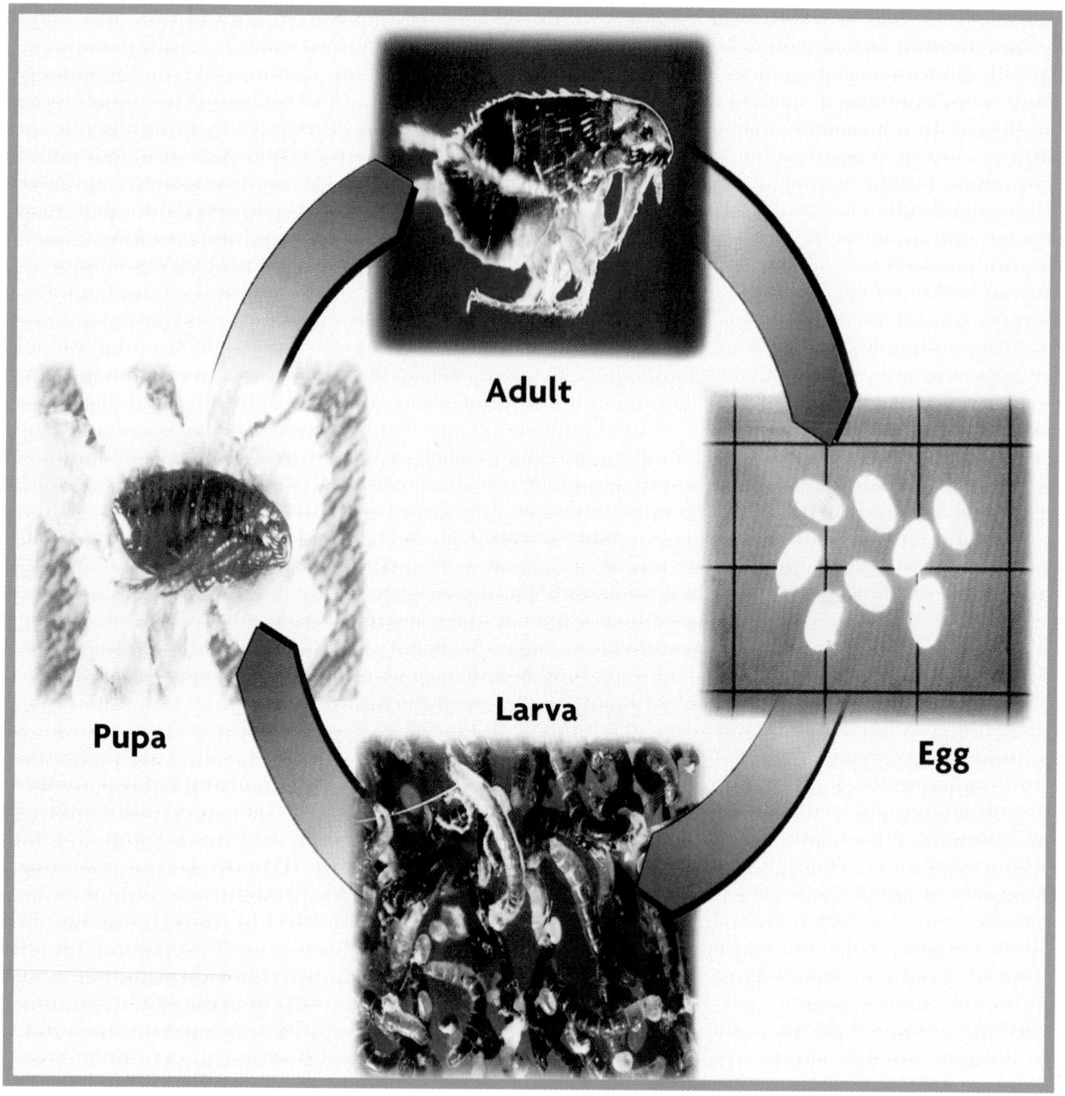


**The life cycle of the flea was posterised by Fleabusters®. Poster courtesy of Fleabusters®, $R_x$ for Fleas.**

cycle and this is why the majority of flea-control products concentrate on this stage. The fact is that adult fleas account for only 1% of the total flea population, and the other 99% exist in pre-adult stages, i.e. eggs, larvae and pupae. The pre-adult stages are barely visible to the naked eye.

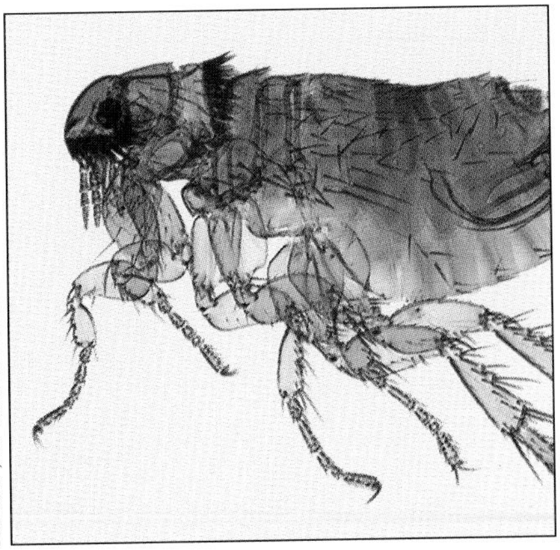

Photo by Jean Claude Revy/Phototake.

**A male dog flea, *Ctenocephalides canis*.**

## On Guard: Catching Fleas Off Guard

Consider the following ways to arm yourself against fleas:

- Add a small amount of pennyroyal or eucalyptus oil to your dog's bath. These natural remedies repel fleas.
- Supplement your dog's food with fresh garlic (minced or grated) and a hearty amount of brewer's yeast, both of which ward off fleas.
- Use a flea comb on your dog daily. Submerge fleas in a cup of bleach to kill them quickly.
- Confine the dog to only a few rooms to limit the spread of fleas in the home.
- Vacuum daily...and get all of the crevices! Dispose of the bag every few days until the problem is under control.
- Wash your dog's bedding daily. Cover cushions where your dog sleeps with towels, and wash the towels often.

### The Life Cycle of the Flea

Eggs are laid on the dog, usually in quantities of about 20 or 30, several times a day. The female adult flea must have a blood meal before each egg-laying session. When first laid, the eggs will cling to the dog's fur, as the eggs are still moist. However, they will quickly dry out and fall from the dog, especially if the dog moves around or scratches. Many eggs will fall off in the dog's favourite area or an area in which

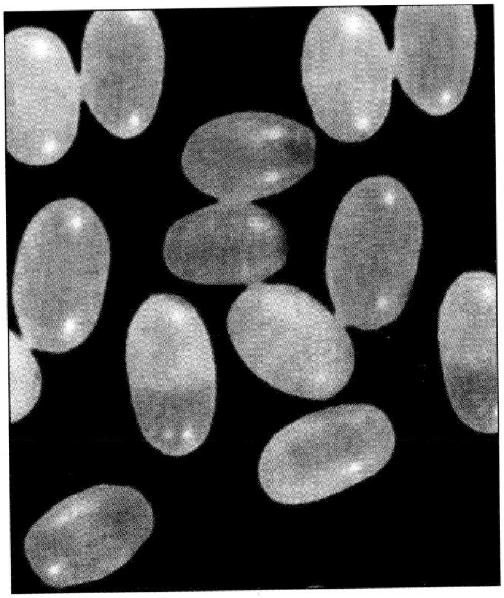

**The eggs of the dog flea.**

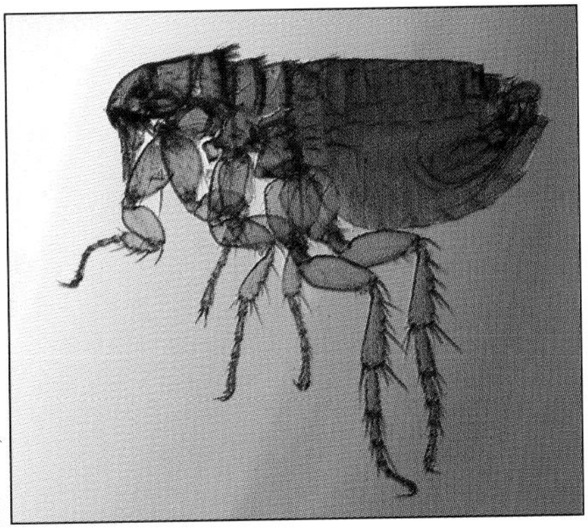

Photo by Jean Claude Revy/Phototake.

**Male cat fleas, *Ctenocephalides felis*, are very commonly found on dogs.**

he spends a lot of time, such as his bed.

Once the eggs fall from the dog onto the carpet or furniture, they will hatch into larvae. This takes from one to ten days. Larvae are not particularly mobile, and will usually travel only a few inches from where they hatch. However, they do have a tendency to move away from light and heavy traffic—under furniture and behind doors are common places to find high quantities of flea larvae.

The flea larvae feed on dead organic matter, including adult flea faeces, until they are ready to change into adult fleas. Fleas will usually remain as larvae for around seven days. After this period, the larvae will pupate into protective pupae. While inside the pupae, the larvae will undergo metamorphosis and change into adult fleas. This can take as little time as a few days, but the adult fleas can remain inside the pupae waiting to hatch for up to two years. The pupae are signalled to hatch by certain stimuli, such as physical pressure—the pupae's being stepped on, heat from an animal lying on the pupae or increased carbon dioxide levels and vibrations—indicating that a suitable host is available.

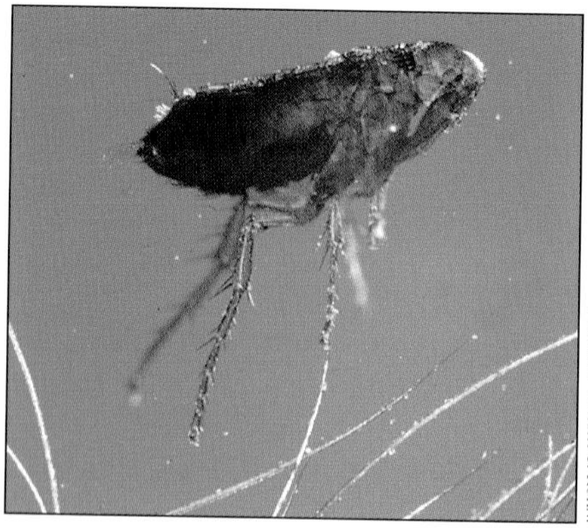

Dwight R Kuhn's magnificent action photo showing a flea jumping from a dog's back.

PHOTO BY DWIGHT R KUHN.

Once hatched, the adult flea must feed within a few days. Once the adult flea finds a host, it will not leave voluntarily. It only becomes dislodged by grooming or the host animal's scratching. The adult flea will remain on the host for the duration of its life unless forcibly removed.

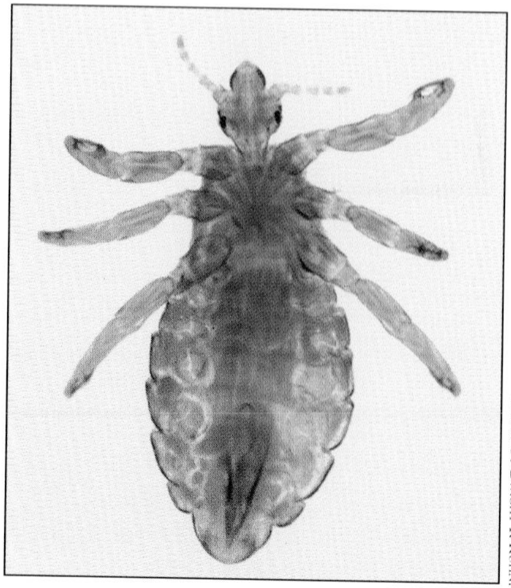

Human lice look like dog lice; the two are closely related.

PHOTO BY DWIGHT R KUHN.

### TREATING THE ENVIRONMENT AND THE DOG

Treating fleas should be a two-pronged attack. First, the environment needs to be treated; this includes carpets and furniture,

## Did You Know?

Never mix flea control products without first consulting your veterinary surgeon. Some products can become toxic when combined with others and can cause serious or fatal consequences.

especially the dog's bedding and areas underneath furniture. The environment should be treated with a household spray containing an Insect Growth Regulator (IGR) and an insecticide to kill the adult fleas. Most IGRs are effective against eggs and larvae; they actually mimic the fleas' own hormones and stop the eggs and larvae from developing into adult fleas. There are currently no treatments available to attack the pupa stage of the life cycle, so the adult insecticide is used to kill the newly hatched adult fleas before they find a host. Most IGRs are active for many months, whilst adult insecticides are only active for a few days.

When treating with a household spray, it is a good idea to vacuum before applying the product. This stimulates as many pupae as possible to hatch into adult fleas. The vacuum cleaner should also be treated with a flea treatment to prevent the eggs and larvae that have been hoovered into the vacuum bag from hatching.

The second stage of treatment is to apply an adult insecticide to the dog. Traditionally, this would be in the form of a collar or a spray, but more recent innovations include digestible insecticides that poison the fleas when they ingest the dog's blood. Alternatively, there are drops that, when placed on the back of the animal's neck, spread throughout the fur and skin to kill adult fleas.

## Did You Know?

Two types of products should be used when treating fleas—a product to treat the pet and a product to treat the home. Adult fleas represent less than 1% of the flea population. The pre-adult fleas (eggs, larvae and pupae) represent more than 99% of the flea population and are found in the environment; it is in the case of pre-adult fleas that products containing an Insect Growth Regulator (IGR) should be used in the home.

IGRs are a new class of compounds used to prevent the development of insects. They do not kill the insect outright, but instead use the insect's biology against it to stop it from completing its growth. Products that contain methoprene are the world's first and leading IGRs. Used to control fleas and other insects, this type of IGR will stop flea larvae from developing and protect the house for up to seven months.

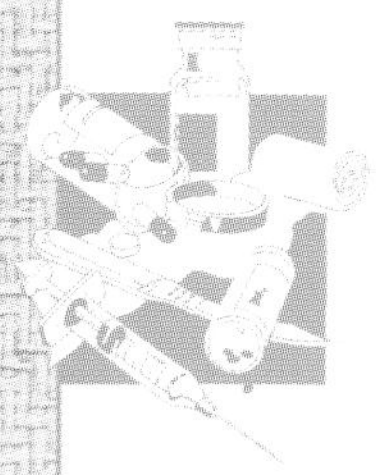

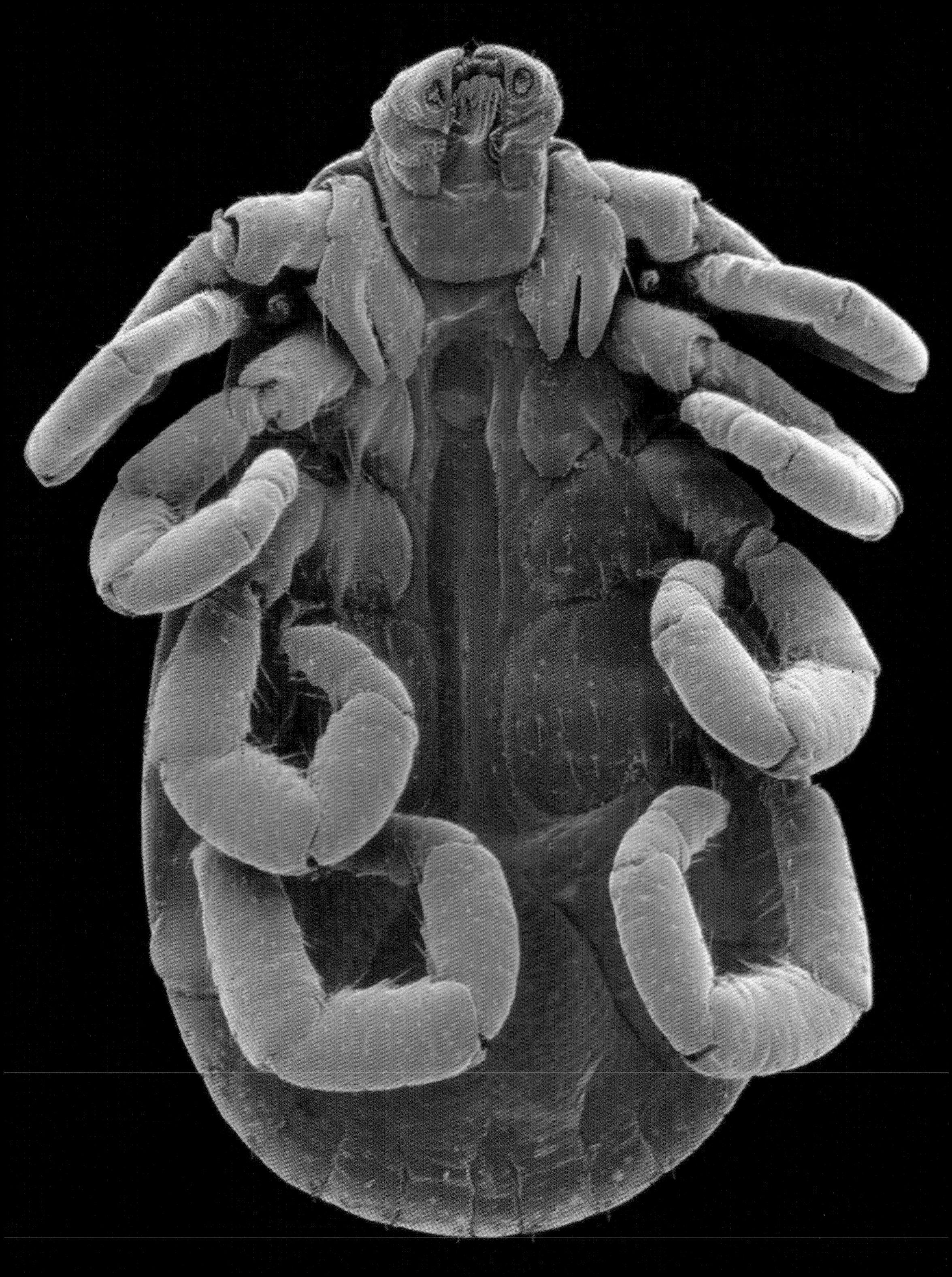

### Ticks and Mites

Though not as common as fleas, ticks and mites are found all over the tropical and temperate world. They don't bite, like fleas; they harpoon. They dig their sharp proboscis (nose) into the dog's skin and drink the blood. Their only food and drink is dog's blood. Dogs can get Lyme disease, Rocky Mountain spotted fever (normally found in the USA only), paralysis and many other diseases from ticks and mites. They may live where fleas are found and they like to hide in cracks or seams in walls wherever dogs live. They are controlled the same way fleas are controlled.

The dog tick, *Dermacentor variabilis*, may well be the most common dog tick in many geographical areas, especially those areas where the climate is hot and humid.

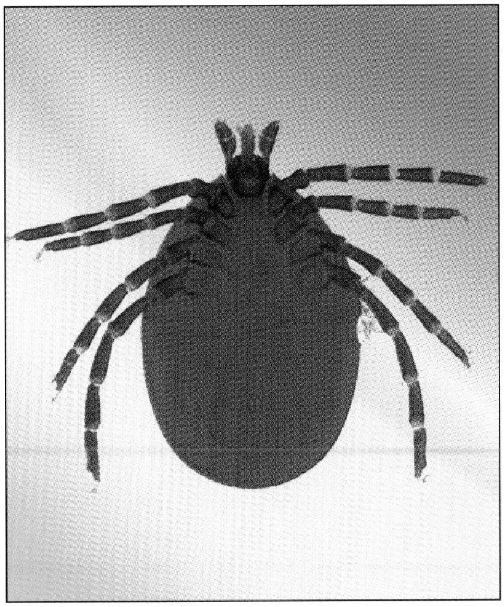

Photo by Jean Claude Revy/Phototake

**An uncommon dog tick of the genus *Ixode*. Magnified 10x.**

**Opposite page: The dog tick, *Dermacentor variabilis*, is probably the most common tick found on dogs. Look at the strength in its eight legs! No wonder it's hard to detach them.**

Most dog ticks have life expectancies of a week to six months, depending upon climatic conditions. They can neither jump nor fly, but they can crawl slowly and can range up to 5 metres (16 feet) to reach a sleeping or unsuspecting dog.

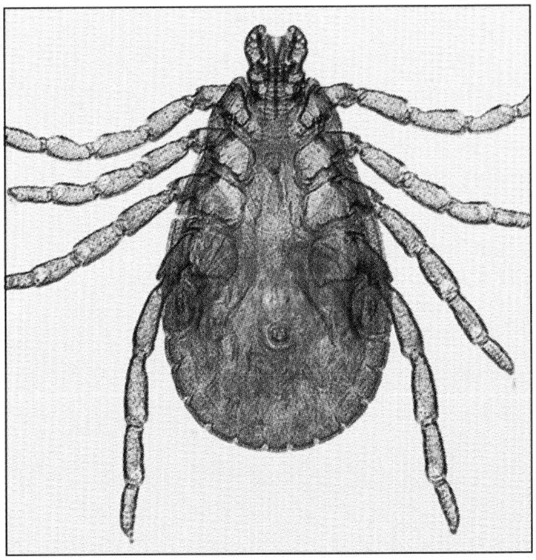

Photo by Carolina Biological Supply/Phototake.

S.E.M. by Dr Dennis Kunkel, University of Hawaii

**A brown dog tick, *Rhipicephalus sanguineus*, is an uncommon but annoying tick found on dogs.**

### Mange

Mites cause a skin irritation called mange. Some are contagious, like *Cheyletiella*, ear mites, scabies and chiggers. Mites that cause ear-mite infestations are usually controlled with ivermectin, which is often toxic to Collies and should be avoided in herding breeds.

It is essential that your dog be treated for mange as quickly as possible because some forms of mange are transmissible to people.

Two views of the mange mite, ***Psoroptes bovis.***

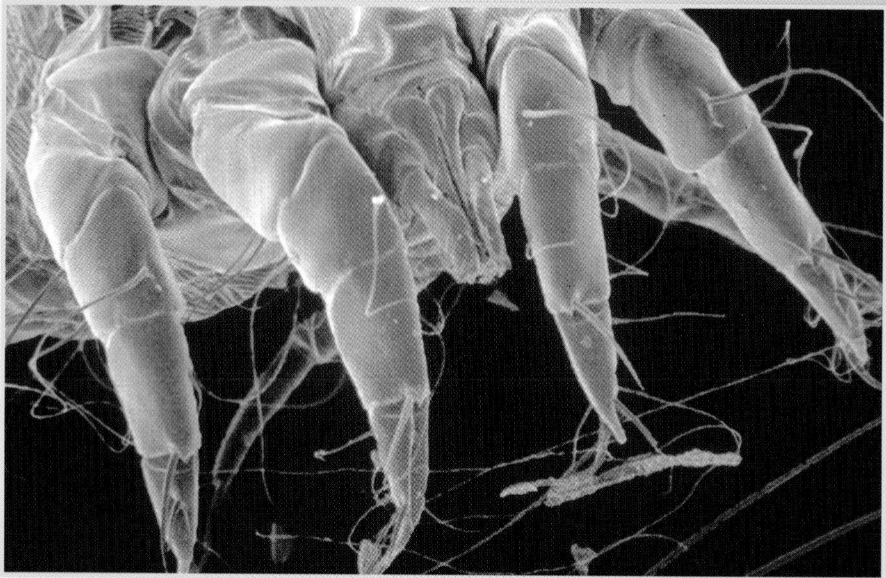
SEM by James Hayden-Yoav/Phototake

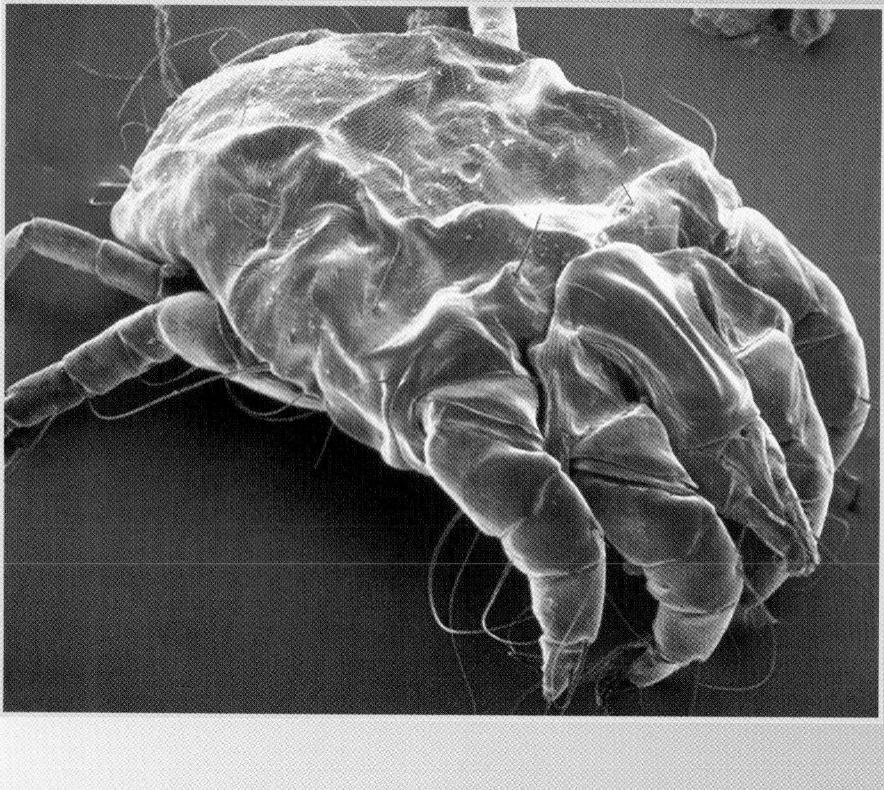
SEM by James Hayden-Yoav/Phototake

## INTERNAL PARASITES

Most animals—fishes, birds and mammals, including dogs and humans—have worms and other parasites that live inside their bodies. According to Dr Herbert R Axelrod, the fish pathologist, there are two kinds of parasites: dumb and smart. The smart parasites live in peaceful cooperation with their hosts (symbiosis), while the dumb parasites kill their host. Most of the worm infections are relatively easy to control. If they are not controlled they eventually weaken the host dog to the point that other medical problems occur, but they are not dumb parasites.

### ROUNDWORMS

The roundworms that infect dogs are scientifically known as *Toxocara canis*. They live in the dog's intestine. The worms shed eggs continually. It has been estimated that a dog produces about 150 grammes of faeces every day. Each gramme of faeces averages 10,000–12,000 eggs of roundworms. There are no known areas in which dogs roam that do not contain roundworm eggs. The greatest danger of roundworms is

## Did You Know?

Ridding your puppy of worms is VERY IMPORTANT because certain worms that puppies carry, such as tapeworms and roundworms, can infect humans.

Breeders initiate a deworming programme at or about four weeks of age. The routine is repeated every two or three weeks until the puppy is three months old. The breeder from whom you obtained your puppy should provide you with the complete details of the deworming programme.

Your veterinary surgeon can prescribe and monitor the programme of deworming for you. The usual programme is treating the puppy every 15–20 days until the puppy is positively worm free.

It is not advised that you treat your puppy with drugs that are not recommended professionally.

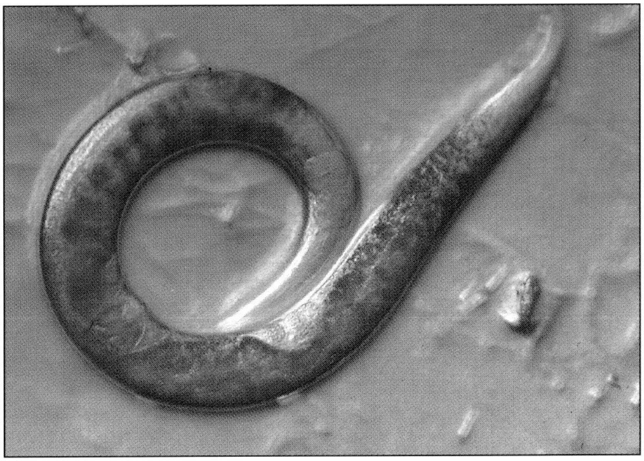

PHOTO BY CAROLINA BIOLOGICAL SUPPLY/PHOTOTAKE.

**The roundworm, *Rhabditis*. The roundworm can infect both dogs and humans.**

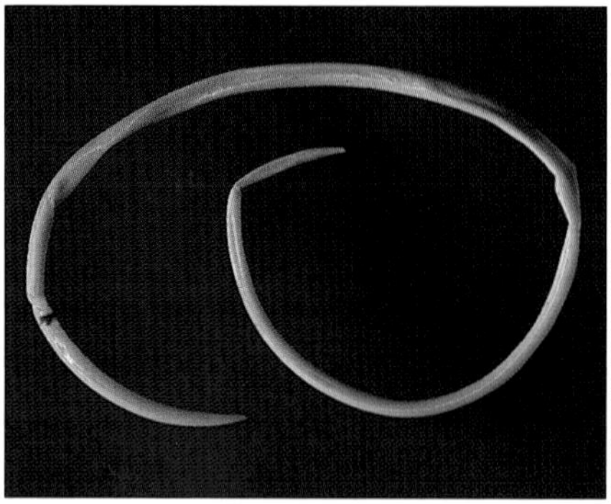

**The roundworm *Rhabditis*.**

PHOTO BY CAROLINA BIOLOGICAL SUPPLY/PHOTOTAKE.

that they infect people too! It is wise to have your dog tested regularly for roundworms.

Pigs also have roundworm infections that can be passed to humans and dogs. The typical roundworm parasite is called *Ascaris lumbricoides*.

### HOOKWORMS

The worm *Ancylostoma caninum* is commonly called the dog hookworm. It is dangerous to humans and cats. It also has teeth by which it attaches itself to the intestines of the dog. It changes the site of its attachment about six times a day and the dog loses blood from each detachment, possibly causing iron-deficiency anaemia. Hookworms are easily purged from the dog with many medications. Milbemycin oxime, which also serves as a heartworm preventative in Collies, can be used for this purpose.

In Britain the 'temperate climate' hookworm (*Uncinaria stenocephala*) is rarely found in pet or show dogs, but can occur in hunting packs, racing Greyhounds and sheepdogs because the worms can be prevalent wherever dogs are exercised regularly on grassland.

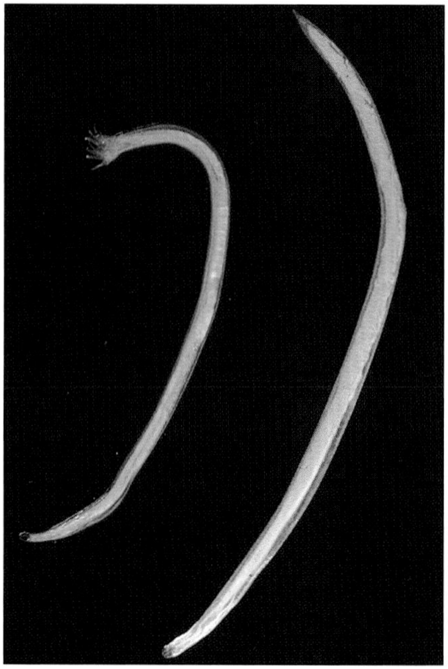

**Male and female hookworms, *Ancylostoma caninum*, are uncommonly found in pet or show dogs in Britain. Hookworms may infect other dogs that have exposure to grasslands.**

PHOTO BY DWIGHT R KUHN.

## Did You Know?

Caring for the puppy starts before the puppy is born by keeping the dam healthy and well-nourished. Most puppies have worms, even if they are not evident, so a worming programme is essential. The worms continually shed eggs except during their dormant stage, when they just rest in the tissues of the puppy. During this stage they are not evident during a routine examination.

## Did You Know?

Average size dogs can pass 1,360,000 roundworm eggs every day.

For example, if there were only 1 million dogs in the world, the world would be saturated with 1,300 metric tonnes of dog faeces.

These faeces would contain 15,000,000,000 roundworm eggs.

7–31% of home gardens and children's play boxes in the U. S. contain roundworm eggs.

Flushing dog's faeces down the toilet is not a safe practice because the usual sewage treatments do not destroy roundworm eggs.

Infected puppies start shedding roundworm eggs at 3 weeks of age. They can be infected by their mother's milk.

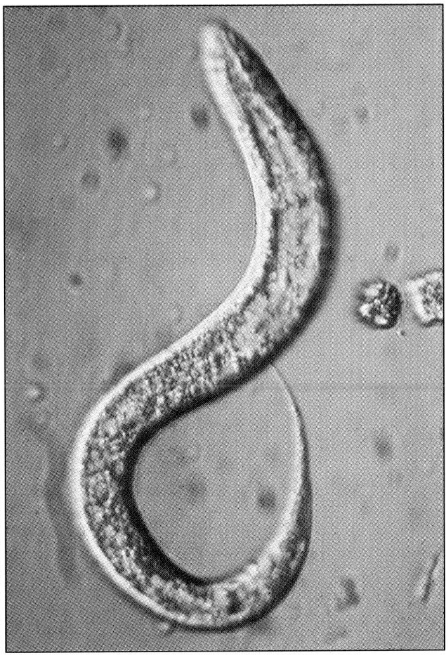

Photo by C James Webb/Phototake.

The infective stage of the hookworm larva.

### Tapeworms

There are many species of tapeworms. They are carried by fleas! The dog eats the flea and starts the tapeworm cycle. Humans can also be infected with tapeworms, so don't eat fleas! Fleas are so small that your dog could pass them onto your hands, your plate or your food and thus make it possible for you to ingest a flea which is carrying tapeworm eggs.

While tapeworm infection is not life threatening in dogs (smart parasite!), it can be the cause of a very serious liver disease for humans. About 50 percent of the humans infected with

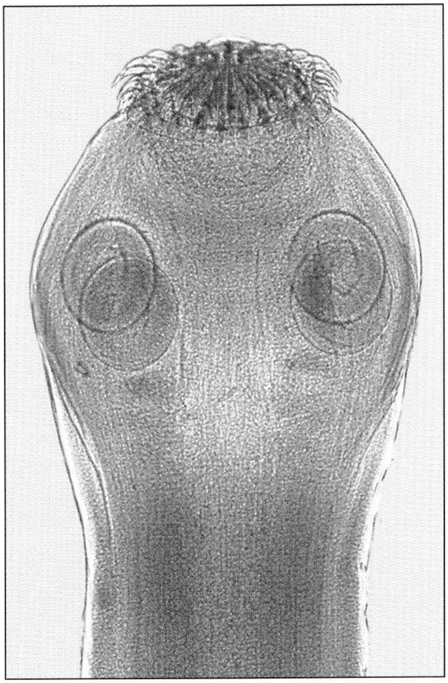

Photo by Carolina Biological Supply/Phototake.

The head and rostellum (the round prominence on the scolex) of a tapeworm, which infects dogs and humans.

*Echinococcus multilocularis*, a type of tapeworm that causes alveolar hydatis, perish.

**HEARTWORMS**

Heartworms are thin, extended worms up to 30 cms (12 ins) long which live in a dog's heart and the major blood vessels surrounding it. Dogs may have up to 200 of these worms. The symptoms may be loss of energy, loss of appetite, coughing, the development of a pot belly and anaemia.

Heartworms are transmitted by mosquitoes. The mosquito drinks the blood of an infected dog and takes in larvae with the blood. The larvae, called microfilaria, develop within the body of the mosquito and are passed on to the next dog bitten after the larvae mature. It takes two to three weeks for the larvae to develop to the infective stage within the body of the mosquito. Dogs should be treated at about six weeks of age, then every six months.

Blood testing for heartworms is not necessarily indicative of how seriously your dog is infected. This is a dangerous disease. Although heartworm is a problem for dogs in America, Australia, Asia and Central Europe, dogs in the United Kingdom are not affected by heartworm.

## Did You Know?

Humans, rats, squirrels, foxes, coyotes, wolves, mixed breeds of dogs and purebred dogs are all susceptible to tapeworm infection. Except in humans, tapeworms are usually not a fatal infection.

Infected individuals can harbour a thousand parasitic worms.

Tapeworms have two sexes—male and female (many other worms have only one sex—male and female in the same worm).

If dogs eat infected rats or mice, they get the tapeworm disease.

One month after attaching to a dog's intestine, the worm starts shedding eggs. These eggs are infective immediately.

Infective eggs can live for a few months without a host animal.

Roundworms, whipworms and tapeworms are just a few of the other commonly known worms that infect dogs.

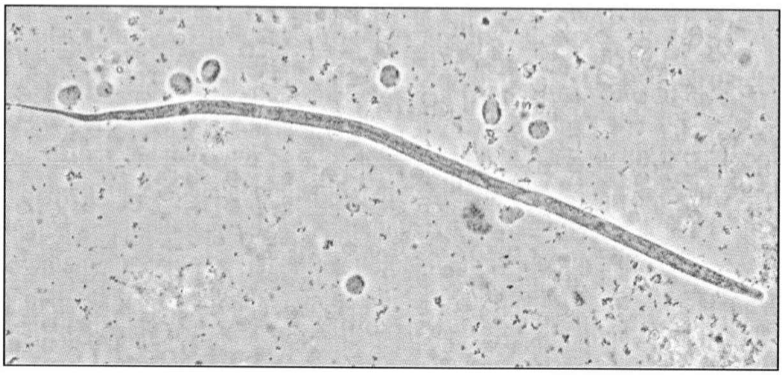

**The heartworm, *Dirofilaria immitis*.**

PHOTO BY JAMES E HAYDEN, RPB/PHOTOTAKE

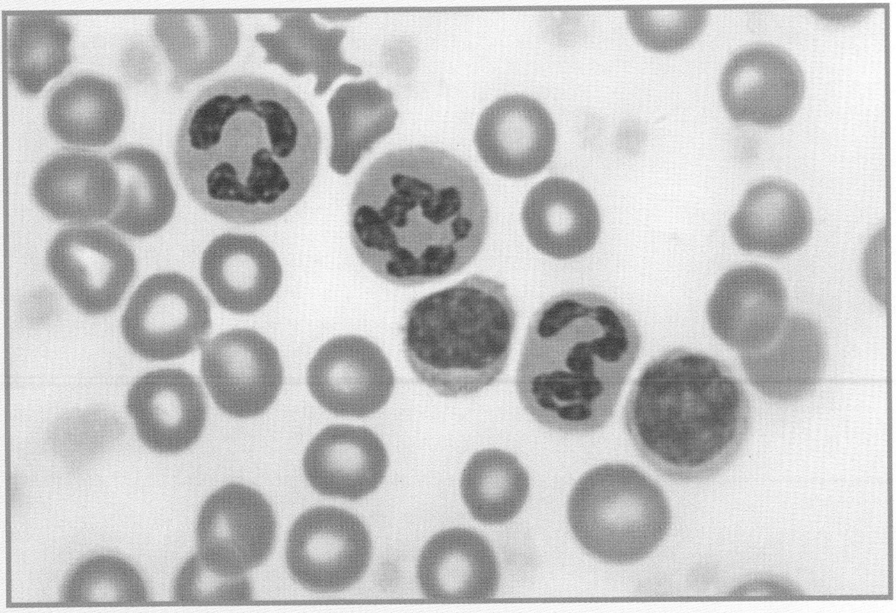

PHOTO BY CAROLINA BIOLOGICAL SUPPLY/PHOTOTAKE.

**Magnified heartworm larvae, *Dirofilaria immitis.***

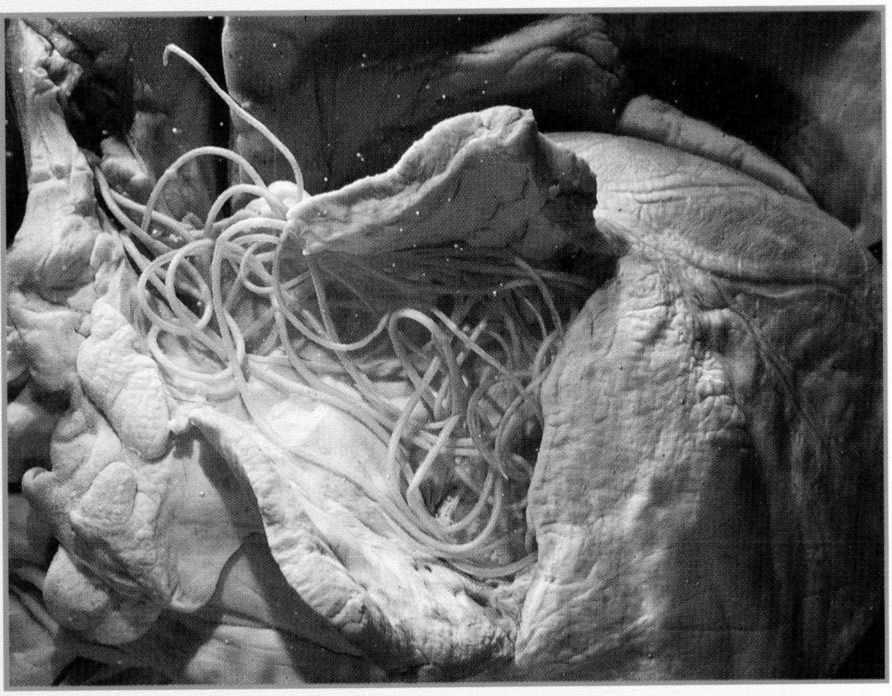

PHOTO BY JAMES E HAYDEN, RPB/PHOTOTAKE.

**The heart of a dog infected with canine heartworm, *Dirofilaria immitis.***

# DO YOU KNOW ABOUT HIP DYSPLASIA?

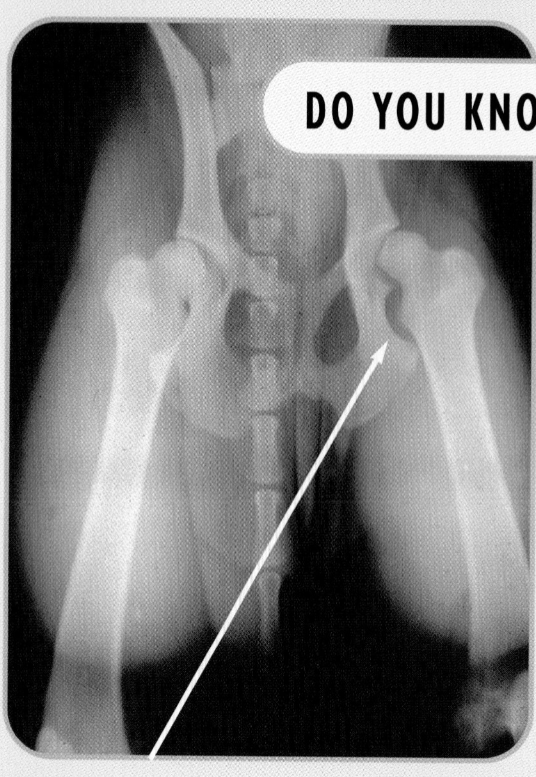

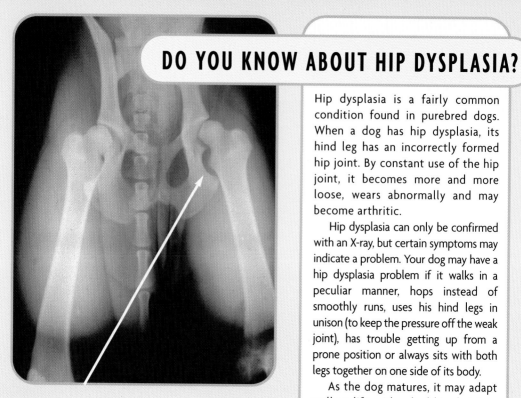

Hip dysplasia is a fairly common condition found in purebred dogs. When a dog has hip dysplasia, its hind leg has an incorrectly formed hip joint. By constant use of the hip joint, it becomes more and more loose, wears abnormally and may become arthritic.

Hip dysplasia can only be confirmed with an X-ray, but certain symptoms may indicate a problem. Your dog may have a hip dysplasia problem if it walks in a peculiar manner, hops instead of smoothly runs, uses his hind legs in unison (to keep the pressure off the weak joint), has trouble getting up from a prone position or always sits with both legs together on one side of its body.

As the dog matures, it may adapt well to life with a bad hip, but in a few years the arthritis develops and many dogs with hip dysplasia become cripples.

Hip dysplasia is considered an inherited disease and can usually be diagnosed when the dog is three to nine months old. Some experts claim that a special diet might help your puppy outgrow the bad hip, but the usual treatments are surgical. The removal of the pectineus muscle, the removal of the round part of the femur, reconstructing the pelvis and replacing the hip with an artificial one are all surgical interventions that are expensive, but they are usually very successful. Follow the advice of your veterinary surgeon.

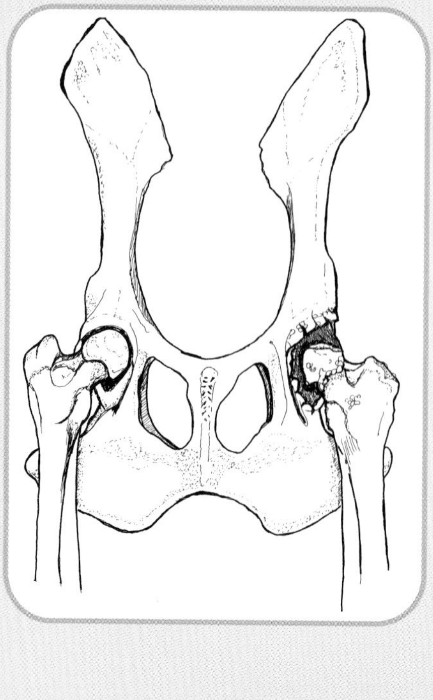

**Hip dysplasia is a badly worn hip joint caused by improper fit of the bone into the socket. It is easily the most common hip problem in larger dogs. The illustration shows a healthy hip joint on the left and an unhealthy hip joint on the right.**

# CDS: COGNITIVE DYSFUNCTION SYNDROME

## 'OLD DOG SYNDROME'

There are many ways for you to evaluate old-dog syndrome. Veterinary surgeons have defined CDS (cognitive dysfunction syndrome) as the gradual deterioration of cognitive abilities. These are indicated by changes in the dog's behaviour. When a dog changes its routine response, and maladies have been eliminated as the cause of these behavioural changes, then CDS is the usual diagnosis.

More than half the dogs over 8 years old suffer some form of CDS. The older the dog, the more chance it has of suffering from CDS. In humans, doctors often dismiss the CDS behavioural changes as part of 'winding down.'

There are four major signs of CDS: frequent toilet accidents inside the home, sleeps much more or much less than normal, acts confused and fails to respond to social stimuli.

### SYMPTOMS OF CDS

**FREQUENT TOILET ACCIDENTS**

- *Urinates in the house.*
- *Defecates in the house.*
- *Doesn't signal that he wants to go out.*

**SLEEP PATTERNS**

- *Moves much more slowly.*
- *Sleeps more than normal during the day.*
- *Sleeps less during the night.*
- *Walks around listlessly and without a destination goal.*

**CONFUSION**

- *Goes outside and just stands there.*
- *Appears confused with a faraway look in his eyes.*
- *Hides more often.*
- *Doesn't recognise friends.*
- *Doesn't come when called.*

**FAILS TO RESPOND TO SOCIAL STIMULI**

- *Comes to people less frequently, whether called or not.*
- *Doesn't tolerate petting for more than a short time.*
- *Doesn't come to the door when you return home from work.*

# YOUR SENIOR PARSON JACK RUSSELL TERRIER

An older Jack Russell will not be as active as he was in puppyhood.

The term old is a qualitative term. For dogs, as well as their masters, old is relative. Certainly we can all distinguish between a puppy Jack Russell and an adult Jack Russell—there are the obvious physical traits, such as size, appearance and facial expressions, and personality traits. Puppies that are nasty are very rare. Puppies and young dogs like to play with children. Children's natural exuberance is a good match for the seemingly endless energy of young dogs. They like to run, jump, chase and retrieve. When dogs grow up and cease their interaction with children, they are often thought of as being too old to play with the kids.

On the other hand, if a Jack Russell is only exposed to people over 60 years of age, its life will normally be less active and it will not seem to be getting old as its activity level slows down.

If people live to be 100 years old, dogs live to be 20 years old. Whilst this is a good rule of thumb, it is very inaccurate. When trying to compare dog years to human years, you cannot make a generalisation about all dogs. Terriers as a whole are long-lived dogs and your Jack Russell will be no different. If your dog lives to 8 years of age, he will often last until 12 years of age. Give your dog his yearly inoculations, visit the veterinary surgeon as needed, feed him a good diet and give him plenty of exercise and your dog should live a long life with you

## Did You Know?

The bottom line is simply that a dog is getting old when YOU think it is getting old because it slows down in its general activities, including walking, running, eating, jumping and retrieving. On the other hand, certain activities increase, such as more sleeping, more barking and more repetition of habits like going to the door without being called when you put your coat on to leave or go outdoors.

and give you much pleasure.

Dogs are generally considered mature within three years, but they can reproduce even earlier. So the first three years of a dog's life are like seven times that of comparable humans. That means a 3-year-old dog is like a 21-year-old human. As the curve of comparison shows, there is no hard and fast rule for comparing dog and human ages. The comparison is made even more difficult, for not all humans age at the same rate...and human females live longer than human males.

## WHAT TO LOOK FOR IN SENIORS

Most veterinary surgeons and behaviourists use the seventh year mark as the time to consider a dog a 'senior.' The term 'senior' does not imply that the dog is geriatric and has begun to fail in mind and body. Ageing is essentially a slowing process. Humans readily admit that they feel a difference in their activity level from age 20 to 30, and then from 30 to 40, etc. By treating the seven-year-old dog as a senior, owners are able to implement certain therapeutic and preventive medical strategies with the help of their veterinary surgeons. A senior-care programme should include at least two veterinary visits per year, screening sessions to determine the dog's health status, as well as nutritional counselling.

### Information . . .

**An old dog starts to show one or more of the following symptoms:**

- **The hair on its face and paws starts to turn grey. The colour breakdown usually starts around the eyes and mouth.**
- **Sleep patterns are deeper and longer and the old dog is harder to awaken.**
- **Food intake diminishes.**
- **Responses to calls, whistles and other signals are ignored more and more.**
- **Eye contacts do not evoke tail wagging (assuming they once did).**

Veterinary surgeons determine the senior dog's health status through a blood smear for a complete blood count, serum chemistry profile with electrolytes, urinalysis, blood pressure check, electrocardiogram, ocular tonometry (pressure on the eyeball), and dental prophylaxis.

Such an extensive programme for senior dogs is well advised before owners start to see the obvious physical signs of ageing, such as slower and inhibited movement, greying, increased sleep/nap periods and disinterest in play and other activity. This preventative programme promises a longer, healthier life for the ageing dog. Amongst the physical problems common in ageing dogs are the loss of sight and hearing, arthritis, kidney and liver failure, diabetes mellitus, heart disease and Cushing's disease (a hormonal disease).

In addition to the physical manifestations discussed, there are some behavioural changes and problems related to ageing dogs. Dogs suffering from hearing or vision loss, dental discomfort or arthritis can become aggressive. Likewise the near-deaf and/or blind dog may be startled more easily and react in an unexpectedly aggressive manner. Seniors suffering from senility can become more impatient and irritable. Housesoiling accidents are associated with loss of mobility, kidney problems, loss of sphincter control as well as plaque accumulation, physiological brain changes and reactions to medications. Older dogs, just like young puppies, suffer from separation anxiety, which can lead to excessive barking, whining, housesoiling and destructive behaviour. Seniors may become fearful of everyday sounds, such as vacuum cleaners, heaters, thunder and passing traffic. Some dogs have difficulty sleeping, due to discomfort, the need for frequent toilet visits and the like.

Owners should avoid spoiling the older dog with too many fatty treats. Obesity is a common

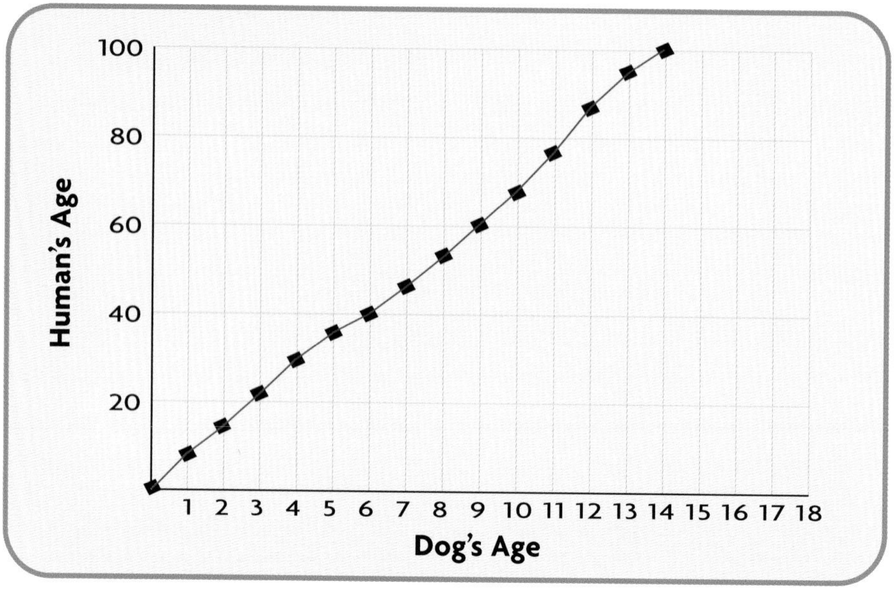

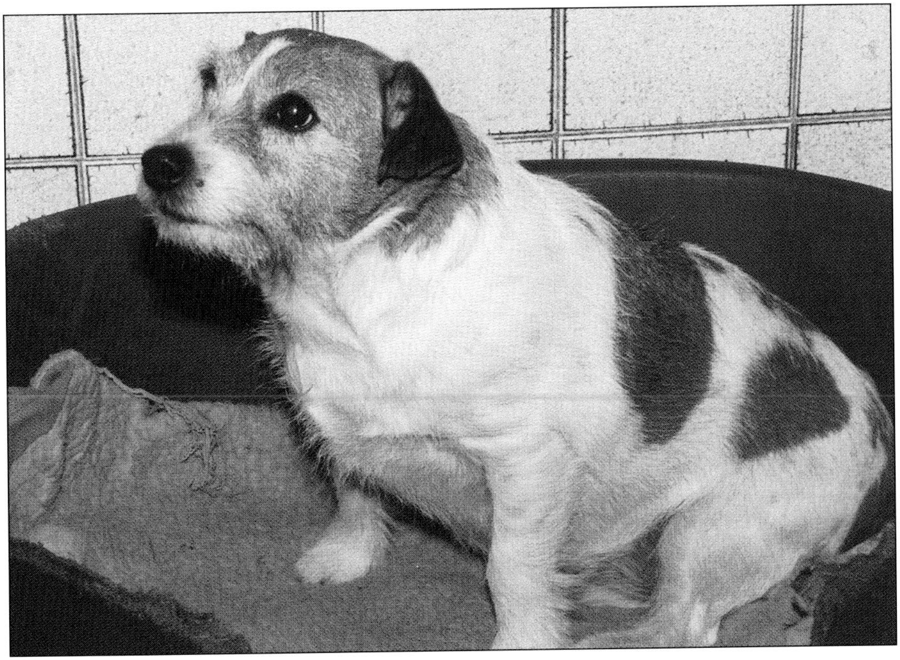

**Senior dogs usually gain excess weight because they are less active. You may find that your senior Jack Russell sleeps for longer periods of time.**

problem in older dogs and subtracts years from their lifespan. Keep the senior dog as trim as possible since excessive weight puts additional stress on the body's vital organs. Some breeders recommend supplementing the diet with foods high in fibre and lower in calories. Adding fresh vegetables and marrow broth to the senior's diet makes a tasty, low-calorie, low-fat supplement. Vets also offer speciality diets for senior dogs that are worth exploring.

Your dog, as he nears his twilight years, needs his owner's patience and good care more than ever. Never punish an older dog for an accident or abnormal behaviour. For all the years of love, protection and companionship that your dog has provided, he deserves special attention and courtesies. The older dog may need to relieve himself at 3 a.m. because he can no longer hold it for eight hours. Older dogs may not be able to remain crated for more than two or three hours. It may be time to give up a sofa or chair to your old friend. Although he may not seem as enthusiastic about your attention and petting, he does appreciate the considerations you offer as he gets older.

Your Jack Russell does not understand why his world is slowing down. Owners must make the transition into the golden

**As your Jack Russell ages, he may benefit from a diet that is specially designed for the older dog to accommodate the changes in his ageing metabolism.**

### Did You Know?

The symptoms listed below are symptoms that gradually appear and become more noticeable. They are not life threatening; however, the symptoms below are to be taken very seriously and a discussion with your veterinary surgeon is warranted:

- Your dog cries and whimpers when it moves and stops running completely.
- Convulsions start or become more serious and frequent. The usual convulsion (spasm) is when the dog stiffens and starts to tremble being unable or unwilling to move. The seizure usually lasts for 5 to 30 minutes.
- Your dog drinks more water and urinates more frequently. Wetting and bowel accidents take place indoors without warning.
- Vomiting becomes more and more frequent.

years as pleasant and rewarding as possible.

## WHAT TO DO WHEN THE TIME COMES

You are never fully prepared to make a rational decision about putting your dog to sleep. It is very obvious that you love your Jack Russell Terrier or you would not be reading this book. Putting a loved dog to sleep is extremely difficult. It is a decision that must be made with your veterinary surgeon. You are usually forced to make the decision when one of

the life-threatening symptoms listed above becomes serious enough for you to seek medical (veterinary) help.

If the prognosis of the malady indicates the end is near and your beloved pet will only suffer more and experience no enjoyment for the balance of its life, then euthanasia is the right choice.

### What is Euthanasia?

Euthanasia derives from the Greek meaning *good death*. In other words, it means the planned, painless killing of a dog suffering from a painful, incurable condition, or who is so aged that it cannot walk, see, eat or control its excretory functions.

Euthanasia is usually accomplished by injection with an overdose of an anaesthesia or barbiturate. Aside from the prick of the needle, the experience is usually painless.

### Making the Decision

The decision to euthanize your dog is never easy. The days during which the dog becomes ill and the end occurs can be unusually stressful for you. If this is your first experience with the death of a loved one, you may need the comfort dictated by your religious beliefs. If you are the head of the family and have children, you should have involved them in the decision of putting your Jack Russell to sleep. Usually your dog can be maintained on drugs for a few days in order to give you ample time to make a decision. During this time, talking with members of your family or even

**You probably can find a lovely pet cemetery near your home. Your veterinary surgeon can usually recommend such a facility.**

## Did You Know?

Euthanasia must be done by a licensed veterinary surgeon. There also may be societies for the prevention of cruelty to animals in your area. They often offer this service upon a vet's recommendation.

people who have lived through this same experience can ease the burden of your inevitable decision.

**THE FINAL RESTING PLACE**

Dogs can have some of the same privileges as humans. They can be buried in a pet cemetery, which is generally expensive, or if they have died at home can be buried in your garden in a place suitably marked with some stone or newly planted tree or bush. Alternatively they can be cremated and the ashes returned to you, or some people prefer to leave their dogs at the surgery for the vet's attention. All of these options should be discussed frankly and openly with your veterinary surgeon. Do not be afraid to ask financial questions. Cremations can be individual, but a less expensive option is mass cremation, although of course the ashes can not then be returned. Vets can usually arrange cremation services on your behalf, but you must be aware that in Britain if your dog has died at the surgery the vet cannot legally allow you to take your dog's body home.

**GETTING ANOTHER DOG?**

The grief of losing your beloved dog will be as lasting as the grief of losing a human friend or relative. In most cases, if your dog died of old age (if there is such a thing), it had slowed down considerably. Do you want a new Jack Russell puppy to replace it? Or are you better off in finding a more mature Jack Russell, say two to three years of age, which will usually be housetrained and will have an already developed personality. In this case, you can find out if you like each other after a few hours of being together.

The decision is, of course, your own. Do you want another Jack Russell or perhaps a different breed so as to avoid comparison with your beloved friend? Most people usually buy the same breed because they know (and love) the characteristics of that breed. Then, too, they often know people who have the same breed and perhaps they are lucky enough that a breeder they know and respect expects a litter soon. What could be better?

**Did You Know?**

The more open discussion you have about the whole stressful occurrence, the easier it will be for you when the time comes.

# SHOWING YOUR
# PARSON JACK RUSSELL TERRIER

When you purchased your Parson Jack Russell Terrier, you should have made it clear to the breeder whether you wanted one just as a loveable companion and pet, or if you hoped to be buying a Jack Russell with show prospects. No reputable breeder will sell you a young puppy saying that it is definitely of show quality, for so much can go wrong during the early weeks and months of a puppy's development. If you plan to show, what you will hopefully have acquired is a puppy with 'show potential.'

To the novice, exhibiting a Jack Russell in the show ring may look easy but it usually takes a lot of hard work and devotion to do top winning at a show such as the prestigious Crufts, not to mention a little luck too!

## Did You Know?

The Kennel Club divides its dogs into seven Groups: Gundogs, Utility, Working, Toy, Terrier, Hounds and Pastoral.*

**The Pastoral Group, established in 1999, includes those sheepdog breeds previously categorised in the Working Group.*

The first concept that the canine novice learns when watching a dog show is that each breed first competes against members of its own breed. Once

**There is simply no greater pleasure for an owner of a fine Parson Jack Russell Terrier than to win a dog show.**

the judge has selected the best member of each breed, provided that the show is judged on a Group system, that chosen dog will compete with other dogs in its group. Finally, the best of each group will compete for Best in Show and Reserve Best in Show.

The second concept that you must understand is that the dogs are not actually being compared to one another. The judge compares each dog against the breed standard, which is a written description of the ideal specimen

## Winning the Ticket

Earning a championship at Kennel Club shows is the most difficult in the world. Compared to the United States and

Canada where it is relatively not 'challenging,' collecting three green tickets not only requires much time and effort, it can be very expensive! Challenge Certificates, as the tickets are properly known, are the building blocks of champions—good breeding, good handling, good training and good luck!

of the breed. Whilst some early breed standards were indeed based on specific dogs that were famous or popular, many dedicated enthusiasts say that a perfect specimen, described in the standard, has never been bred. Thus the 'perfect' dog never walked into a show ring and, to the woe of dog breeders around the globe, does not exist. Breeders attempt to get as close to this ideal as possible, with every litter, but theoretically the 'perfect' dog is so elusive that it is impossible. (And if the 'perfect' dog were born, breeders and judges would never agree that it was indeed 'perfect.')

If you are interested in exploring dog shows, your best bet is to join your local breed club. These clubs often host both Championship and Open Shows, and sometimes Match meetings and Special Events, all of which could be of interest, even if you are only an onlooker. Clubs also send out newsletters and some organise training days and seminars in order that people may learn more about their chosen breed. To locate the nearest breed club for you, contact The Kennel Club, the ruling body for the British dog world. The Kennel Club governs not only conformation shows but also working trials, obedience trials, agility trials and field trials. The Kennel Club furnishes the rules and regulations for all these events plus general dog registration and other basic requirements of dog ownership. Its annual show called the Crufts Dog Show, held in Birmingham, is the largest bench show in England. Every year around 20,000 of the U.K.'s best dogs qualify to participate in this marvellous show which lasts four days.

The Kennel Club governs many different kinds of shows in Great Britain, Australia, South Africa and beyond. At the most competitive and prestigious of these shows, the Championship Shows, a dog can earn Challenge Certificates, and thereby become a Show Champion or a Champion. A dog must earn three Challenge Certificates under three different judges to earn the prefix of 'Sh Ch' or 'Ch'. Note that some breeds must also qualify in a field trial in order to gain the title of full champion. Challenge Certificates are awarded to a very small percentage of the dogs competing, especially as dogs which are already Champions compete with others for these coveted CCs. The number of Challenge Certificates awarded in any one year is based upon the total number of dogs in each breed entered for competition. There are three types of Championship Shows: an all-breed General Championship show for all Kennel-Club-recognised breeds; a Group Championship Show, limited to breeds within one of the groups; and a Breed Show, usually confined to a single breed. The Kennel Club determines which breeds at which Championship Shows will have the opportunity to earn Challenge Certificates (or tickets). Serious exhibitors often will opt not to participate if the tickets are withheld at a particular show. This policy makes earning

## Show Ring Etiquette

**Just as with anything else, there is a certain etiquette to the show ring that can only be learned through experience. Showing your dog can be quite intimidating to you as a**

**novice when it seems as if everyone else knows what they are doing. You can familiarise yourself with ring procedure beforehand by taking a class to prepare you and your dog for conformation showing or by talking with an experienced handler. When you are in the ring, listen and pay attention to the judge and follow his/her directions. Remember, even the most skilled handlers had to start somewhere. Keep it up and you too will become a proficient handler before too long!**

Winners of most dog shows are rewarded with medals, ribbons and cups of various sizes. There are rarely cash awards, but dogs who win prizes are more valued as breeding animals.

championships ever more difficult to accomplish.

Open Shows are generally less competitive and are frequently used as 'practice shows' for young dogs. There are hundreds of Open Shows each year that can be invitingly social events and are great first show experiences for the novice. Even if you're considering just watching a show to wet your paws, an Open Show is a great choice.

Whilst Championship and Open Shows are most important for the beginner to understand, there are other types of shows in which the interested dog owner can participate. Training clubs sponsor Matches that can be entered on the day of the show for a nominal fee. In these introductory-level exhibitions, two dogs are pulled out of a hat and 'matched,' the winner of that match goes on to the next round, and eventually only one dog is left undefeated.

Exemption Shows are much more light-hearted affairs with usually only four pedigree classes and several 'fun' classes, all of which can be entered on the day. The proceeds of an Exemption Show must be given to a charity and are sometimes held in conjunction with small agricultural shows. Limited Shows are also available in small number, but entry is restricted to members of the club which hosts the show, although one can usually join the club when making an entry.

Before you actually step into the ring, you would be well advised to sit back and observe the judge's ring procedure. If it is your first time in the ring, do not be over-anxious and run to the front of the line. It is much better to stand back and study how the exhibitor in front of you is performing. The judge asks each handler to 'stand' the dog, hopefully showing the dog off to his best advantage. The judge will observe the dog from a distance and from different angles, approach the dog, check his teeth, overall structure, alertness and muscle tone, as well as consider how well the dog 'conforms' to the standard. Most importantly, the judge will have the exhibitor move the dog around the ring in some pattern that he or she should specify (another advantage to not going first, but always listen since some judges change their directions, and the judge is always right!) Finally the judge will give the dog one last look before moving on to the next exhibitor.

If you are not in the top three at your first show, do not be discouraged. Be patient and consistent and you may eventually find yourself in the winning lineup. Remember that the winners were once in your shoes and have devoted many hours and much money to earn the placement. If you find that your dog is losing every time and never getting a nod, it may be time to consider a different dog sport or just enjoy your Jack Russell as a pet.

**WORKING TRIALS**

Working trials can be entered by any well-trained dog of any breed, not just Gundogs or Working dogs. Many dogs that earn the Kennel Club Good Citizen Dog award choose to participate in a working

## Classes at Dog Shows

There can be as many as 18 classes per sex for your breed. Check the show schedule carefully to make sure that you have entered your dog in the appropriate class. Among the classes offered can be: Beginners; Minor Puppy (ages 6 to 9

months); Puppy (ages 6 to 12 months); Junior (ages 6 to 18 months); Beginners (handler or dog never won first place) as well as the following, each of which is defined in the schedule: Maiden; Novice; Tyro; Debutant; Undergraduate; Graduate; Postgraduate; Minor Limit; Mid Limit; Limit; Open; Veteran; Stud Dog; Brood Bitch; Progeny; Brace and Team.

**Jack Russell Terriers are very agile dogs and, since they train easily, many are seen at agility trials.**

trial. There are five stakes at both open and championship levels: Companion Dog (CD), Utility Dog (UD), Working Dog (WD), Tracking Dog (TD) and Patrol Dog (PD). As in conformation shows, dogs compete against a standard and if the dog reaches the qualifying mark, it obtains a certificate. Divided into groups, each exercise must be achieved 70 percent in order to qualify. If the dog achieves 80 percent in the open level, it receives a Certificate of Merit (COM), in the championship level, it receives a Qualifying Certificate. At the CD stake, dogs must participate in four groups, Control, Stay, Agility and Search (Retrieve and Nosework). At the next three levels, UD, WD and TD, there are only three groups: Control, Agility and Nosework.

Agility consists of three jumps: a vertical scale up a wall of planks; a clear jump over a basic hurdle with a removable top bar; and a long jump across angled planks.

To earn the UD, WD and TD, dogs must track approximately one-half mile for articles laid from one-half hour to three hours ago. Tracks consist of turns and legs, and fresh ground is used for each participant.

The fifth stake, PD, involves teaching manwork, which is not recommended for every breed.

## FIELD TRIALS AND WORKING TESTS

Working tests are frequently used to prepare dogs for field trials, the purpose of which is to heighten the instincts and natural abilities of gundogs. Live game is not used in working tests. Unlike field trials, working tests do not count toward a dog's record at The Kennel Club, though the same judges often oversee working tests. Field trials began in England in 1947 and are only moderately popular amongst dog folk. Whilst breeders of Working and Gundog breeds concern themselves with the field abilities of their dogs, there is considerably less interest in field trials than dog shows. In order for dogs to become full champions, certain breeds must qualify in the field as well. Upon gaining three CCs in the show ring, the dog is designated a Show Champion (Sh Ch). The title Champion (Ch) requires that the dog gain an award at a field trial, be a 'special qualifier' at a field trial or pass a 'special show dog qualifier' judged by a field trial judge on a shooting day.

### How to Enter a Dog Show

1. Obtain an entry form and show schedule from the Show Secretary.

2. Select the classes that you want to enter and complete the entry form.
3. Transfer your dog into your name at The Kennel Club. (Be sure that this matter is handled before entering.)
4. Find out how far in advance show entries must be made. Oftentimes it's more than a couple of months.

## AGILITY TRIALS

Agility trials began in the United Kingdom in 1977 and have since spread around the world, especially to the United States, where agility enjoys strong popularity. The handler directs his dog over an obstacle course that includes jumps (such as those used in the working trials), as well as tyres, the dog walk, weave poles, pipe tunnels, collapsed tunnels, etc. The Kennel Club requires that dogs not be trained for agility until they are 12

**Active and athletic, this Jack Russell clears a bar jump at an agility trial with ease.**

months old. This dog sport intends to be great fun for dog and owner and interested owners should join a training club that has obstacles and experienced agility handlers who can introduce you and your dog to the 'ropes' (and tyres, tunnels and so on).

## FÉDÉRATION CYNOLOGIQUE INTERNATIONALE

Established in 1911, the Fédération Cynologique Internationale (FCI) represents the 'world kennel club.' This international body brings uniformity to the breeding, judging and showing of purebred dogs. Although the FCI originally included only four European nations: France, Holland, Austria and Belgium (which remains its headquarters), the organisation today embraces nations on six continents and recognises well over 300 breeds of purebred dog. There are three titles attainable through the FCI: the International Champion, which is the most prestigious; the International Beauty Champion, which is based on aptitude certificates in different countries; and the International Trial Champion, which is based on achievement in obedience trials in different countries. Quarantine laws in England and Australia prohibit most of their exhibitors from entering FCI shows. The rest of the Continent does participate in these impressive canine spectacles, the largest of which is the World Dog Show, hosted in a different country each year. FCI sponsors both national and international shows. The hosting country determines the judging system and breed standards are always based on the breed's country of origin.

# UNDERSTANDING THE BEHAVIOUR OF YOUR PARSON JACK RUSSELL TERRIER

As a Parson Jack Russell Terrier owner, you have selected your dog so that you and your loved ones can have a companion, a protector, a friend and a four-legged family member. You invest time, money and effort to care for and train the family's new charge. Of course, this chosen canine behaves perfectly! Well, perfectly like a dog.

**THINK LIKE A DOG**

Dogs do not think like humans, nor do humans think like dogs, though we try. Unfortunately, a dog is incapable of figuring out how humans think, so the responsibility falls on the owner to adopt a proper canine mindset. Dogs cannot rationalise, and dogs exist in the present moment. Many dog owners make the mistake in training of thinking that they can reprimand their dog for something he did a while ago. Basically, you cannot even reprimand a dog for something he did 20 seconds ago! Either catch him in the act or forget it! It is a waste of your and your dog's time—in his mind, you are reprimanding him for whatever he is doing at that moment.

The following behavioural problems represent some which owners most commonly encounter. Every dog is unique and every situation is unique. No author could purport to solve your Jack Russell's problem simply by reading a script. Here we outline some basic 'dogspeak' so that owners' chances of solving

**Did You Know?**

Dogs left alone for varying lengths of time may often react wildly when you return. Sometimes they run, jump, bite,

chew, tear things apart, wet themselves, gobble their food or behave in a very undisciplined manner. Allow them to calm down before greeting them or they will consider your attention as a reward for their antics.

## Information . . .

**Physical games like pulling contests, wrestling, jumping and teasing should not be encouraged. Inciting the dog's crazy behaviour tends to confuse a dog. The owner has to**

**be able to control his dog at all times; even in play, your dog has to know that you're the leader. He should never be allowed to act aggressively in play.**

behavioural problems are increased. Discuss bad habits with your veterinary surgeon and he/she can recommend a behavioural specialist to consult in appropriate cases. Since behavioural abnormalities are the leading reason owners abandon their pets, we hope that you will make a valiant effort to solve your Jack Russell's problem. Patience and understanding are virtues that dwell in every pet-loving household.

### AGGRESSION

This is the most obvious problem that concerns owners of Jack Russells. Aggression can be a very big problem in dogs, and, when not controlled, always becomes dangerous. An aggressive dog, no matter the size, may lunge at, bite or even attack a person or another dog. Aggressive behaviour is not to be tolerated. It is more than just inappropriate behaviour; it is not safe, no matter what the breed. It is painful for a family to watch their dog become unpredictable in his behaviour to the point where they are afraid of him. Whilst not all aggressive behaviour is dangerous, growling, baring teeth, etc., can be frightening. It is important to ascertain why the dog is acting in this manner. Aggression is a display of dominance, and the dog should not have the dominant role in its pack, which is, in this case, your family.

It is important not to challenge an aggressive dog as this could provoke an attack. Observe your Jack Russell's body language. Does he make direct eye contact and stare? Does he try to make himself as large as possible: ears pricked, chest out, tail erect? Height and size signify authority in a dog pack—being taller or 'above' another dog literally means that he is 'above' in the social status. These body signals tell you that your Jack Russell thinks he is in charge, a problem that needs to be addressed. An aggressive dog is unpredictable: you never know when he is going to strike and what he is going to do. You cannot understand why a dog that is playful and loving one minute is growling and snapping the next.

The best solution is to consult a behavioural specialist, one who has experience with the Jack Russell if possible. Together, perhaps you can pinpoint the cause of your dog's aggression and do something about it. An aggressive dog cannot be trusted, and a dog that cannot be trusted is not safe to have as a family pet. If, very unusually, you find that your pet has become untrustworthy and you feel it necessary to seek a new home with a more suitable family and environment, explain fully to the new owners all your reasons for rehoming the dog to be fair to all concerned. In the very worst case, you will have to consider euthanasia.

### Aggression Toward Other Dogs

A dog's aggressive behaviour toward another dog sometimes stems from insufficient exposure to other dogs at an early age. If other dogs make your Jack Russell nervous and agitated, he will lash out as a defensive mechanism, though this behaviour is thankfully uncommon in the breed. A dog who has not received sufficient exposure to other canines tends to believe that he is the only dog on the planet. The animal becomes so dominant that he does not even show signs that he is fearful or threatened. Without growling or any other physical signal as a warning, he will lunge at and bite the other dog. A way to correct this is to let your Jack Russell approach another dog when walking on lead. Watch very closely and at the very first sign of aggression, correct your Jack Russell and pull him away. Scold him for any sign of discomfort, and then praise him when he ignores or tolerates the other dog. Keep this up until he stops the aggressive behaviour, learns to ignore the other dog or accepts other dogs. Praise him lavishly for his correct behaviour.

**Dogs use their mouths for many reasons besides eating. The dog on the left is expressing affection but the dog on the right wants no part of it.**

### Dominant Aggression

A social hierarchy is firmly established in a wild dog pack. The dog wants to dominate those under him and please those above him. Dogs know that there must be a leader. If you are not the obvious choice for emperor, the dog will assume the throne! These conflicting innate desires are what a dog owner is up against when he sets about training a dog. In training a dog to obey commands, the owner is reinforcing that he is the top dog in the 'pack' and that the dog should, and should want to, serve his superior. Thus, the owner is suppressing the dog's urge to dominate by modifying his behaviour and making him obedient.

An important part of training is taking every opportunity to reinforce that you are the leader. The simple action of making your Jack Russell sit to wait for his food says that you control when he eats and that he is dependent on you for food. Although it may be difficult, do not give in to your dog's wishes every time he whines at you or looks at you with his pleading eyes. It is a constant effort to show the dog that his place in the pack is at the bottom. This is not meant to sound cruel or inhumane. You love your Jack Russell and you should treat him with care and affection. You (hopefully) did not get a dog just so you could boss around another creature. Dog training is not about being cruel or feeling important, it is about moulding the dog's behaviour into what is acceptable and teaching him to live by your rules. In theory, it is quite simple: catch him in appropriate behaviour and reward him for it. Add a dog into the equation and it becomes a bit more trying, but as a rule of thumb, positive reinforcement is what works best.

With a dominant dog, punishment and negative reinforcement can have the opposite effect of what you are after. It can make a dog fearful and/or act out aggressively if he feels he is being challenged. Remember, a dominant dog perceives himself at the top of the social heap and will fight to defend his perceived status. The best way to prevent that is never to give him reason to think that he is in control in the first place. If you are having trouble training your Jack Russell and it seems as if he is constantly challenging your authority, seek the help of an obedience trainer or behavioural specialist. A professional will work with both you and your dog to teach you effective techniques to use at home. Beware of trainers who rely on excessively harsh methods; scolding is necessary now and then, but the focus in your training should always be on positive reinforcement.

If you can isolate what brings out the fear reaction, you can help the dog get over it. Supervise your Jack Russell's interactions with people and other dogs, and praise the dog when it goes well. If he starts to act aggressively in a situation, correct him and remove him from the situation. Do not let people approach the dog and start petting him without your express permission. That way, you can have the dog sit to accept petting, and praise him when he behaves properly. You are focusing on praise and on modifying his behaviour by rewarding him when he acts appropriately. By being gentle and by supervising his interactions, you are showing him that there is no need to be afraid or defensive.

### SEXUAL BEHAVIOUR

Dogs exhibit certain sexual behaviours that may have influenced your choice of male or female when you first purchased your Jack Russell. To a certain extent, spaying/neutering will eliminate these behaviours, but if you are purchasing a dog that you wish to breed, you should be aware of what you will have to deal with throughout the dog's life.

Female dogs usually have two oestruses per year with each season lasting about three weeks. These are the only times in which a female dog will mate, and she usually will not allow this until the second week of the cycle, but this does vary from bitch to bitch. If not bred during the heat cycle, it is not uncommon for a bitch to experience a false pregnancy, in which her mammary glands swell and she exhibits maternal tendencies toward toys or other objects.

Owners must further recognise that mounting is not merely a sexual expression but also one of dominance. Be consistent and persistent and you will find that you can 'move mounters.'

### CHEWING

The national canine pastime is chewing! Every dog loves to sink his 'canines' into a tasty bone, but sometimes that bone is attached to his owner's hand! Dogs need to chew, to massage their gums, to make their new teeth feel better and to exercise their jaws. This is a natural behaviour deeply imbedded in all things canine. Our role as owners is not to stop the dog's chewing, but to redirect it to positive, chew-worthy objects. Be an informed owner and purchase proper chew toys like strong nylon bones that will not splinter. Be sure that the devices are safe and durable, since your dog's safety is at risk. Again, the owner is responsible for ensuring a dog-proof environment. The best answer is prevention: that is, put your shoes, handbags and other tasty objects in their proper places (out of the reach of the growing canine mouth). Direct puppies to their toys whenever you see them tasting the furniture legs or the leg of your trousers. Make a loud noise to attract the pup's attention and immediately escort him to his chew toy and engage him with the

Dogs are at their happiest when they can roll on their backs, wiggle...and smile. Dogs may be the only animals (besides humans) that can smile.

toy for at least four minutes, praising and encouraging him all the while.

Some trainers recommend deterrents, such as hot pepper or another bitter spice or a product designed for this purpose, to discourage the dog from chewing unwanted objects. Test out these products yourself before investing in a large quantity.

### JUMPING UP

Jumping up is a dog's friendly way of saying hello! Some dog owners do not mind when their dog jumps up, which is fine for them. The problem arises when guests come to the house and the dog greets them in the same manner—whether they like it or not! However friendly the greeting may be, the chances are that your visitors will not appreciate your dog's enthusiasm. The dog will not be able to distinguish upon whom he can jump and whom he cannot. Therefore, it is probably best to discourage this behaviour entirely.

Pick a command such as 'Off.' (avoid using 'Down' since you will use that for the dog to lie down) and tell him 'Off' when he jumps up. Place him on the ground on all fours and have him sit, praising him the whole time. Always lavish him with praise and petting when he is in the sit position. That way you are still giving him a warm affectionate greeting, because you are as excited to see him as he is to see you!

### DIGGING

Digging, which is seen as a destructive behaviour to humans, is actually quite a natural behaviour in dogs, especially terriers, and their desire to dig can be irrepressible and most frustrating to owners. When digging occurs in your garden, it is actually a normal behaviour redirected into something the dog can do in his everyday life. In the wild, a dog would be actively seeking food, making his own shelter, etc. He would be using his paws in a purposeful manner for his survival. Since you provide him with food and shelter, he has no need to use his paws for these purposes, and so the energy that he would be using may manifest itself in the form of little holes all over your garden and flower beds.

Perhaps your dog is digging as a reaction to boredom—it is somewhat similar to someone eating a whole bag of crisps in front of the TV—because they are there and there is not anything better to do! Basically, the answer is to provide the dog with adequate play and exercise so that his mind and paws are occupied, and so that he feels as if he is doing something useful.

Of course, digging is easiest to control if it is stopped as soon as possible, but it is often hard to catch a dog in the act. If your dog is a compulsive digger and is not easily distracted by other activities, you can designate an area on your property where it is okay for him to dig. If you catch him digging in an off-limits area of the garden, immediately bring him to the approved area and praise him for digging there. Keep a close eye on him so that you can catch him in the act—that is the only way to make him understand what is permitted and what is not. If you take him to a hole he dug an hour ago and tell him 'No,' he will understand that you are not fond of holes, or dirt, or flowers. If you catch him whilst he is stifle-deep in your tulips, that is when he will get your message.

**BARKING**

Dogs cannot talk—oh, what they would say if they could! Instead, barking is a dog's way of 'talking.' It can be somewhat frustrating because it is not always easy to tell what a dog means by his bark—is he excited, happy, frightened or angry? Whatever it is that the dog is trying to say, he should not be punished for barking. It is only when the barking becomes excessive, and when the excessive barking becomes a bad habit, that the behaviour needs to be modified. Jack Russells are highly vocal, and they tend to use their barks more purposefully than most dogs. If an intruder came into your home in the middle of the night and your Jack Russell barked a warning, wouldn't you be pleased? You would probably deem your dog a hero, a wonderful guardian and protector of the home. Most dogs are not as discriminate as the Jack Russell. For instance, if a friend drops by unexpectedly and rings the doorbell and is greeted with a sudden sharp bark, you would probably be annoyed at the

**No one enjoys living with a food thief. You must train your dog not to steal food.**

dog. But in reality, isn't this just the same behaviour? The dog does not know any better...unless he sees who is at the door and it is someone he knows, he will bark as a means of vocalising that his (and your) territory is being threatened. Whilst your friend is not posing a threat, it is all the same to the dog. Barking is his means of letting you know that there is an intrusion, whether friend or foe, on your property. This type of barking is instinctive and should not be discouraged.

Excessive habitual barking, however, is a problem that should be corrected early on. As your Jack Russell grows up, you will be able to tell when his barking is purposeful and when it is for no reason. You will become able to distinguish your dog's different barks and their meanings. For example, the bark when someone comes to the door will be different from the bark when he is excited to see you. It is similar to a person's tone of voice, except that the dog has to rely totally on tone of voice because he does not have the benefit of using words. An incessant barker will be evident at an early age.

There are some things that encourage a dog to bark. For example, if your dog barks non-stop for a few minutes and you give him a treat to quiet him, he believes that you are rewarding him for barking. He will associate barking with getting a treat, and will keep doing it until he is rewarded.

## FOOD STEALING

Is your dog devising ways of stealing food from your coffee table? If so, you must answer the following question: Is your Jack Russell hungry, or is he 'constantly famished' like many dogs seem to be? Face it, some dogs are more food-motivated than others. Some dogs are totally obsessed with the smell of food and can only think of their next meal. Food stealing is terrific fun and always yields a great reward—FOOD, glorious food.

The owner's goal, therefore, is to be sensible about where food is placed in the home, and to reprimand your dog whenever he is caught in the act of stealing. But remember, only reprimand the dog if you actually see him stealing, not later when the crime is discovered for that will be of no use at all and will only serve to confuse.

**BEGGING**

Just like food stealing, begging is a favourite pastime of hungry puppies! It yields that same lovely reward—FOOD! Dogs quickly learn that their owners keep the 'good food' for themselves, and that we humans do not dine on dried food alone. Begging is a conditioned response related to a specific stimulus, time and place. The sounds of the kitchen, cans and bottles opening, crinkling bags, the smell of food in preparation, etc., will excite the dog and soon the paws are in the air!

Here is the solution to stopping this behaviour: Never give in to a beggar! You are rewarding the dog for sitting pretty, jumping up, whining and rubbing his nose into you by giving him that glorious reward—food. By ignoring the dog, you will (eventually) force the behaviour into extinction. Note that the behaviour is likely to get worse before it disappears, so be sure there are not any 'softies' in the family who will give in to little 'Oliver' every time he whimpers, 'More, please.'

**SEPARATION ANXIETY**

Your Jack Russell may howl, whine or otherwise vocalise his displeasure at your leaving the house and his being left alone. This is a normal reaction, no different from the child who cries as his mother leaves him on the first day at school. In fact, constant attention can lead to separation anxiety in the first place. If you are endlessly fussing over your dog, he will come to expect this from you all of the time and it will be more traumatic for him when you are not there. Obviously, you enjoy spending time with your dog, and he thrives on your love and attention. However, it should not become a dependent relationship where he is heartbroken without you.

One thing you can do to minimise separation anxiety is to make your entrances and exits as low-key as possible. Do not give your dog a long drawn-out goodbye, and do not overly lavish him with hugs and kisses when you return. This is giving in to the attention that he craves, and it will only make him miss it more when you are away. Another thing you can try is to give your dog a treat when you leave; this will not only keep him occupied and keep his mind off the fact that you have just left, but it will also help him associate your leaving with a pleasant experience.

You may have to accustom your dog to being left alone in intervals. Of course, when your dog starts whimpering as you approach the door, your first instinct will be to run to him and comfort him, but do not do it! Really—eventually he will adjust and be just fine if you take it in small steps.

# INDEX

*Page numbers in **boldface** indicate illustrations.*

# My Parson Jack Russell Terrier

PUT YOUR PUPPY'S FIRST PICTURE HERE

Dog's Name ______________________________

Date ____________ Photographer ______________________